The Liberator

The Story of William Lloyd Garrison

CIVIL RIGHTS LEADERS

A. Philip Randolph

Bayard Rustin

Ella Baker

Frederick Douglass

Harvey Milk

Ida B. Wells Barnett

Roy Wilkins

W. E. B. Du Bois

William Lloyd Garrison

The Liberator

The Story of William Lloyd Garrison

MORGAN REYNOLDS
PUBLISHING

Greensboro, North Carolina

The Liberator: The Story of William Lloyd Garrison

Library of Congress Cataloging-in-Publication Data

Esty, Amos.
 The liberator : the story of William Lloyd Garrison / by Amos Esty. -- 1st ed.
    p. cm. -- (Civil rights leaders)
 Includes bibliographical references and index.
 ISBN 978-1-59935-137-7 (alk. paper)
1. Garrison, William Lloyd, 1805-1879--Juvenile literature. 2.
Abolitionists--United States--Biography--Juvenile literature. 3.
Antislavery movements--United States--History--19th century--Juvenile
literature. I. Title.
 E449.G25E88 2010
 326'.8092--dc22
 [B]
                                        2009054290

Printed in the United States of America
First edition

Contents

Wm. Lloyd Garrison.

Chapter

1

Growing Up Fast

By mid-afternoon on October 21, 1835, so many people had gathered outside 46 Washington Street in Boston, Massachusetts, that Helen Garrison could not even make her way into the building. She was there to attend a meeting of the Boston Female Anti-Slavery Society, a women's abolitionist organization. Helen Garrison and other abolitionists hoped to convince their fellow citizens to free the 2 million black Americans held as slaves in the South. William Lloyd Garrison, Helen's husband, was scheduled to give a speech to the society, despite rumors that a proslavery mob planned to disrupt the meeting.

Unlike Helen, most of those gathered outside the building were not members of the women's organization. In fact, most were men who opposed abolitionism and were angry at Helen's husband for his outspoken attacks on slavery. As the meeting began, the men started to yell for Garrison to come out and face them. Realizing the danger, Garrison withdrew to a back room. The crowd broke through the doors of the offices to look for him. If captured, Garrison would be tarred and feathered—or worse. He briefly escaped by climbing out a back entrance into an alley and hiding on the second floor of a nearby shop, but it did not take long for the crowd to find him. Several men seized Garrison, tied him loosely with rope, and forced him to descend a ladder to the street below.

As an abolitionist, Garrison had long known that he faced the possibility of violence against him—this was not the first time he had faced a mob—but never before had he been in such danger. Although slavery had been abolished in Massachusetts decades earlier, it was still an important part of the nation's economy, even in the North, and few people questioned whether it was right or wrong to hold slaves. Those who did criticize slavery, such as Garrison, were treated by most Americans as dangerous radicals, and on this day Garrison's crusade put his life at risk. Garrison, however, was willing to take that chance.

In 1805, the year of William Lloyd Garrison's birth, about 1 million Americans were held as slaves in the United States. Lloyd, as he preferred to be called, was born on December 12 in Newburyport, Massachusetts, a busy shipping town north of Boston. His father, Abijah Garrison, and mother, Frances Maria Lloyd Garrison, had moved there from New Brunswick, Canada, just two years earlier. Lloyd was their third child. James Holley Garrison and Caroline Eliza Garrison had been born in 1801 and 1803, respectively.

Lloyd's childhood was not always a happy one. Abijah, a sea pilot, moved the family to Newburyport to try to find better opportunities for work. The town was a bustling center of shipbuilding and trade in the first few years of the nineteenth century, and Abijah found plenty of work on ships headed to the South and to the West Indies. The family lived in rooms rented from David and Martha Farnham. Soon Frances and Martha became good friends, and the two led weekly prayer meetings in the house.

Unfortunately for the Garrisons, much of New England hit hard economic times soon after the family arrived. Within a few years of Lloyd's birth, Abijah found himself unable to obtain work, and he began filling his time with drinking when he should have been looking for employment. His drinking led to tension in the household. Frances had become a strict Baptist as a child after listening to a sermon by a traveling minister, and she disapproved of drinking alcohol. To make matters worse, Lloyd's sister, Caroline, fell sick and died in 1808 after eating a poisonous plant in a neighbor's yard. Frances gave birth to another daughter, Elizabeth, in July 1808, but the death of Caroline was a difficult blow for Abijah and Frances.

Before long, Abijah was almost permanently unemployed, and the less he worked, the more he drank. Finally, Abijah simply left. Lloyd never saw his father again. Frances now had to find a way to care for three young children, despite the fact that she had no job and no money.

The family managed to scrape by for a few years with the help of the Farnhams and charity from the town. Lloyd and his brother, James, sold candy that their mother made and gathered clams from the nearby river. In 1814, Frances decided to move to Lynn, Massachusetts, about thirty miles from Newburyport, to try to find work. She took eleven-year-old James with her, hoping to find him a place as an apprentice to a craftsman. It was a difficult decision for Frances, as she was forced to leave young Elizabeth behind with the Farnhams

Illustration of the birthplace of William Lloyd Garrison
(Courtesy of Stock Montage, Inc./Alamy)

and to send Lloyd to live with an older couple, Ezekiel and Salome Bartlett.

Even in Lynn, however, Frances found it difficult to obtain permanent work, and she struggled to send money back to the Farnhams and Bartletts to pay for the care of her children. Meanwhile, James's apprenticeship did not go well. Other employees introduced him to alcohol, and he began to drink and miss work. Despite these problems, Frances decided in 1815 to have Lloyd come to live in Lynn with her. She soon found him a position as an apprentice to a shoemaker.

In the early nineteenth century, apprenticeships were a common way to train for a career. Boys, usually from about age fourteen to age seventeen, would agree to serve their masters until they turned twenty-one. In return for their labor, the apprentices would be given room and board and learn a trade. After completing the apprenticeship, the young men usually would work for several years as journeymen, going from one shop to another until they had the experience and money to open their own business.

Lloyd had been doing well back in Newburyport. He enjoyed going to school, although it took him some time to learn to write with his right hand. He was naturally left-handed, but his teachers forced him to write with his right hand, rapping him on the knuckles with a ruler when he was caught using his left. He did not like the thought of moving to Lynn and giving up school and his friends to work. It was soon clear that Lloyd did not have much talent for shoemaking. He was small and not very strong, and he grew tired quickly from the difficult manual labor.

That same year, Frances decided to move the family again. She accepted an offer from a local businessman to move to

Baltimore to work for him there in a new factory. In October 1815, she, James, and Lloyd arrived in Baltimore. Elizabeth stayed behind in Newburyport with the Farnhams. At the time, Baltimore was the third-largest city in the country, with nearly 60,000 residents. The change of scenery did not seem to matter to James. He continued to cause trouble with his drinking. After he was quickly fired from two jobs, Frances sent him back to Lynn, hoping that he would reform.

For Frances, getting by in Baltimore proved to be as difficult as life in Lynn. Her employment at the factory soon ended, and she had trouble finding new work. Lloyd performed various small jobs in the factory for a while, but Frances could tell that he was not happy living in Baltimore. He missed his friends and school back in Newburyport. Frances began to worry that he would soon turn to drinking like his father

An 1849 view of Baltimore Harbor from Federal Hill, with the Washington Monument in the background (*Courtesy of Maryland Historical Society*)

and brother if things did not improve, so she sent Lloyd back to Massachusetts.

Lloyd was happy to be heading back home, but this time it was to work, not to go to school. With the help of Ezekiel Bartlett, Frances arranged for Lloyd to begin an apprenticeship to a cabinetmaker named Moses Short who lived in Haverhill, just fifteen miles from Newburyport.

Once again, Lloyd was miserable with the work. After only a few weeks, he packed up his belongings and tried to escape to Newburyport. Moses Short caught him before he made it very far, but Lloyd was so unhappy that Short kindly agreed to release him from his obligations. Soon Lloyd was back with the Bartletts.

Lloyd needed to figure out what he would do with himself. Fortunately for him, he soon found what turned out to be the perfect answer. In October 1818, a local newspaper publisher, Ephraim Allen, advertised for an apprentice to work at his paper, the *Newburyport Herald.* Lloyd applied for the position, and with the help of Ezekiel Bartlett he soon had the job. He agreed that he would work for Allen for seven years. On October 18, Lloyd began what would be a long career in publishing.

At first, Lloyd was afraid he might have made a mistake. He was intimidated by the complex types and machines he would have to use, and he worried that he would never be able to master the trade of printing. But Lloyd was a quick learner. Over the next few years, he worked hard at his job. He also continued his own informal education by reading widely, attending lectures, and following politics. Although Lloyd would never be able to return to school, he learned to write well and argue effectively.

By 1822, Lloyd's hard work had paid off. Ephraim Allen made him foreman of the shop. That same year, Lloyd began to submit essays to the paper under the pseudonym "An Old Bachelor." Lloyd probably used the false name because he was afraid of being embarrassed if Allen disliked the articles. As it turned out, Allen liked the work of "An Old Bachelor" very much and published a number of Lloyd's essays. His first contributions discussed his opinion of women and marriage. He wrote that he was determined to remain a bachelor "and not trouble myself about the ladies."

Lloyd's professional prospects were looking brighter, but the rest of his family continued to struggle. James had left Massachusetts to become a sailor in 1818, and it would be many years before Lloyd saw his brother again. Elizabeth had moved to Baltimore to be with their mother. Frances wrote Lloyd letters asking him to visit and informing him that both she and Elizabeth were ill. Allen refused to let Lloyd take time off to visit, however, and Lloyd did not want to risk losing his position by leaving. In the fall of 1822, Frances wrote Lloyd to tell him that Elizabeth had died. Still, Allen continued to try to prevent Lloyd from leaving, and he said that Lloyd would have to pay for his own replacement while he was gone. Eventually, however, Lloyd was able to convince Allen to let him go. In the summer of 1823, he finally made it to Baltimore.

By the time he arrived, Frances was so ill that Lloyd hardly recognized his mother. He wrote in a letter to Allen that "instead of the tall, robust woman, blooming in health, which I saw last, she is now . . . pined away to almost a skeleton, and unable to walk." After a visit of a few weeks, Lloyd returned to Newburyport. He soon received word that his mother had died on September 3 at the age of forty-five.

Back in Massachusetts, Lloyd continued to dedicate himself to his work at the paper. He wrote essays about politics using pseudonyms, and he surprised even himself with his success. By now he had become active in local politics. He was a staunch supporter of the Federalists, one of the two main political parties at the time (the Democrats were the other major party). He also helped form a literary club and even gave a public speech on the Fourth of July in 1824.

Finally, in December 1825, the day came when Lloyd's long apprenticeship was over. It had not been easy, but after several failed attempts to find a career, Lloyd had stumbled into editing, and he had proved to be well suited for it. Although no one would have guessed just how successful he would be, Lloyd had shown his willingness to work and his ability to write. Those two qualities, combined with his stubbornness and the religious faith he inherited from his mother, would eventually make William Lloyd Garrison a household name. For now, though, it was time to start out on his own.

Illustration of William Lloyd Garrison making an antislavery speech on Boston Common (*Courtesy of Lebrecht Music and Arts Photo Library/Alamy*)

Chapter
2

From Journalist to Abolitionist

Not long after leaving the *Herald,* Garrison bought a local newspaper, the *Essex Courant,* with the help of a loan from Ephraim Allen. He renamed his paper the *Free Press* and published his first issue on March 22, 1826. At the time, papers often associated themselves with political parties and received many of their subscriptions through members and supporters of that party. Garrison, a Federalist, used his paper to promote his political beliefs. The Federalists wanted a stronger federal government, and they disliked the political tactics used by the Democrats to attract voters.

Garrison included more than just politics in the paper. He intended it to be literary, as well, so he reprinted excerpts from the works of writers such as Jonathan Swift and Washington Irving. He also included many poems, including a number that he wrote himself. Although he was never much of a poet, Garrison did have an eye for spotting good poetry. One day, he received some anonymous poems that he thought were quite good. After some effort, he was able to find out who had written them. The author turned out to be a shy young writer named John Greenleaf Whittier. Garrison published a number of Whittier's poems, beginning a long friendship between the two. Whittier would go on to become one of the most famous poets of the nineteenth century, as well as an abolitionist.

Unfortunately, Garrison had more literary ability than business sense. The abrasive tone of his articles and editorials soon drove off many subscribers. This was not the last time that Garrison's refusal to moderate his opinions and language hurt his popularity. Before long, a public dispute with his former employer, Allen, caused Garrison to lose the paper entirely.

On July 4, 1826, fifty years after the writing of the Declaration of Independence, both John Adams and Thomas Jefferson—the second and third U.S. presidents—died. Garrison admired Adams, who had been a Federalist, but he sharply disagreed with the views of Jefferson, a Democrat. Garrison was bothered by the many tributes to Jefferson published in newspapers across the country, and he was especially annoyed by the glowing eulogy written in the *Newburyport Herald* by Ephraim Allen. In response to Allen's article, Garrison wrote an essay that criticized Jefferson, particularly Jefferson's religious beliefs. When Allen responded by chiding Garrison for his inexperience, Garrison could not help himself from attacking Allen's views in his paper.

This dispute helped lead to the end of Garrison's brief tenure as publisher of the *Free Press*. In September, with too few subscribers to continue, Garrison announced that he would sell the paper. Allen, upset at the criticism from his former apprentice, might have played a role in forcing the sale by demanding repayment of the loan he had given Garrison to buy the paper.

Whatever the reason for the sale, Garrison's first venture into publishing his own paper had ended after only six months. He decided to move to Boston, where there were more opportunities to find printing work. For the next year and a half, he worked sporadically in a number of printing offices, but he could not find steady work.

While living in Boston, Garrison became involved in the temperance movement, which was an effort to convince Americans to give up drinking. Alcohol, particularly in the form of whiskey, was cheap and plentiful in the 1820s. The average American drank almost three times as much alcohol as the average American today. Garrison had seen firsthand in his family the damage that alcohol could do, so it is not surprising that he became part of this group of reformers and took the pledge of the American Temperance Society to abstain from drinking.

Garrison also continued to write anonymously to local papers on social and political matters. He wrote one letter to the *Boston Courier* in 1827 in which he criticized the Massachusetts state legislature for considering a bill to create a lottery. Garrison argued that it would cause poor people to spend the little money they had for the dream of becoming wealthy. Even at this early stage of his career, Garrison obviously had a passion for reforming society.

In January 1828, Garrison received a job offer that would allow him to combine his talent for writing with his interest in reform. He became the editor of the *National Philanthropist,* a newspaper intended to promote the temperance movement. Garrison filled the paper with gruesome accounts of the dangers of drinking and printed the ingredients of popular drinks, hoping that this would make people less likely to want to drink them.

In the spring of 1828, Garrison suddenly became involved in another movement. One night, a Quaker antislavery activist named Benjamin Lundy spoke at the rooming house where Garrison lived. A decade earlier, Lundy had given up his career as a businessman to devote his life to abolition after seeing a group of slaves chained together, waiting to be shipped down a river to be sold. He traveled across the North speaking about slavery and edited an antislavery paper, *The Genius of Universal Emancipation,* which he published in Baltimore. Lundy discussed how he had been converted to the fight against slavery. He also said that most slaveholders would prefer to put an end to slavery but just did not know how.

As soon as Garrison heard Lundy speak, he began working discussions of slavery into the *National Philanthropist.* Before long, Garrison decided to leave the paper and dedicate himself to the antislavery cause. By July, Garrison was already helping Lundy organize an antislavery meeting in Boston. They expected that it would not be hard to find others supportive of their efforts, but they found instead that abolition was an unpopular cause.

Slavery had been abolished in Massachusetts when the state drew up its constitution in the 1780s, but even in the 1820s many Bostonians still worried that criticizing slavery would upset Southerners. Most white Americans simply accepted the existence of slavery without questioning it, and few of them were tolerant of those people, such as Lundy and Garrison, who wanted to cause an uproar about the issue. Lundy had convinced a number of slaveholders in the South to free their slaves, but overall the number of slaves continued to grow. Slavery was a deeply entrenched part of the economy and culture in the United States, and that did not seem likely to change anytime in the near future.

Before long, Lundy left Boston. He planned to tour other cities in the North and then return home to Baltimore. That left Garrison unemployed and agitating for a cause that had little support from his fellow citizens. Fortunately for him, that summer a group of Federalists in Bennington, Vermont, offered him a job as editor of a newspaper that they intended to use to promote the reelection of John Quincy Adams as president. Garrison took the job and moved to southern Vermont. He named the paper the *Journal of the Times*, and on October 3, 1828, he published his first issue.

Garrison enthusiastically praised Adams and criticized Adams's opponent, Andrew Jackson, but his mind kept returning to a bigger issue: the fight against slavery. While in Vermont, he started a petition drive that ultimately collected several thousand signatures calling on Congress to abolish slavery in Washington, D.C.

A 1818 portrait of John Quincy Adams by portrait artist Gilbert Stuart *(Courtesy of Library of Congress)*

He also met with Benjamin Lundy again when Lundy stopped near Bennington during a tour of the North. The two men discussed working together on Lundy's antislavery paper, but they did not make any final decision about the matter.

To Garrison's dismay, Andrew Jackson easily won election that fall. Soon, Garrison decided to move on again. He missed Boston, and he never had felt as passionately about politics as he did about abolition. So, after just six months in Vermont, Garrison left the *Journal of the Times* to return to Boston.

Garrison quickly realized that it would be harder to find work than he had thought. He managed to make ends meet by working in temporary positions at various printing offices,

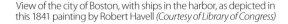

View of the city of Boston, with ships in the harbor, as depicted in this 1841 painting by Robert Havell *(Courtesy of Library of Congress)*

but there were not many opportunities for permanent, full-time work. That summer, however, he had something else to occupy much of his time. A group of local churches invited him to give a speech on the Fourth of July at the famous Park Street Church in Boston.

The country's most prominent antislavery group, the American Colonization Society (ACS) had made a tradition of discussing the topic of slavery on the Fourth of July. The ACS had been formed in 1816 to encourage slaveholders to free their slaves and to help free blacks resettle in Africa. The organization never grew very large, but in the late 1820s it was just about the only group working to end slavery. Local members of the ACS thought that Garrison was a good choice to speak on the subject, so they looked forward to his speech at the Park Street Church. By the end of the day, however, both they and the church group that invited Garrison would deeply regret that decision.

Garrison worked feverishly on the speech, excited to have the chance to speak to such a distinguished audience on this important topic. Of course, he was also nervous. "My very knees knock together at the thought of speaking," he wrote to a friend. Finally the day arrived. Garrison spoke softly at first, but soon he found his voice. He declared that he would not bother to argue that slavery was wrong, as that was obvious. Instead, he said, he would discuss what should be done about it. "Our politics are rotten to the core," he said, and he called for the northern states to do whatever they could to end slavery in the South. He asked his audience what they would do if, "by a miracle, the slaves would suddenly become white. Would you shut your eyes upon their sufferings and calmly talk of constitutional limitations?"

Although his audience was not yet ready to hear such radical statements, Garrison warned that if slavery was not ended, God would eventually punish them for it: "The nation will be shaken as if by a mighty earthquake. . . . Blood will flow like water. . . . The terrible judgments of an incensed God will complete the catastrophe of republican America." Finally, in response to those who argued that it was impossible to abolish slavery, Garrison said that the movement had to start at some point, and that now was as good a time as any. Despite the hopes of the ACS that Garrison would speak in support of their organization, Garrison hardly made any mention of colonization. He had a much more ambitious goal in mind.

Garrison thought his speech had gone well, but few others agreed. The church organization was unlikely to invite him back. Newspapers mostly ignored the speech, and those that did mention it criticized Garrison. In response, he wrote to the *Boston Courier* to defend himself. "It was plain truth told in a plain manner," Garrison wrote. "From my heart, I believe that the moral and political tendency of this nation is downward." A little bit of criticism was not going to discourage Garrison from his new mission.

Not long after Garrison astonished his audience in Boston, he left the city to join Benjamin Lundy in Baltimore to help edit Lundy's paper, *The Genius of Universal Emancipation.* The two agreed that Garrison would take primary responsibility for the paper, which would allow Lundy to continue to travel the country giving antislavery lectures. Although it was Lundy who had inspired Garrison's initial interest in abolition, Garrison's views were more radical than those of Lundy, who supported colonization efforts and believed that emancipation had to occur gradually. Garrison by this time supported immediate emancipation; he thought all the slaves should be freed at once. If slavery was wrong, he argued, why should it be allowed to continue for even one more day?

Despite Garrison's enthusiasm and optimism, slavery was far from ending. In fact, it seemed to be even more important to the nation's growth than ever before. The South produced a large share of the world's supply of cotton, and much of that cotton was used in textile mills in the North. The invention of the steamboat by Robert Fulton in 1807 had tied the economies of the states closer together by allowing cotton and other goods to be carried more easily long distances over canals and rivers. The entire country seemed to be profiting from slavery.

Still, Garrison was not discouraged. The first issue of the paper with Garrison at the helm appeared on September 2, 1829. The paper had an eagle at the top of the page and the motto "*E Pluribus Unum*" just below that. Lundy and Garrison agreed that, because they held slightly different views on some subjects, each would include his initials with his own editorials. The first issue included an editorial by Garrison that called for immediate emancipation. It also included a poem that Garrison published using his old pseudonym from Newburyport, "An Old Bachelor." For the next few months, Garrison wrote more articles criticizing slavery and colonization, and Lundy traveled and made occasional contributions to the paper. Garrison also printed news of some of the horrors of slavery, such as descriptions of slaves who had been murdered or the brutal punishment of runaway slaves who were captured.

In November, Garrison wrote an article noting that a ship owned by Francis Todd, a wealthy merchant who lived in Garrison's hometown of Newburyport, was about to leave the port at Baltimore to bring seventy-five slaves to New Orleans. Garrison criticized Todd for making money from the slave trade. "Any man can gather up riches," Garrison wrote of Todd, "if he does not care by what means they are obtained." In 1808, Congress had outlawed importing slaves directly from Africa to the United States, so the sale of slaves from states in the Upper South, such as Maryland, to the Deep South had become a vital part of the system of slavery.

By pointing out that the ship carrying the slaves was owned by a Northerner, Garrison wanted to implicate the North in slavery. It was not just the South that was guilty. But two months later, in January, Garrison learned that Francis Todd was suing him for libel. Plus, Garrison also would face criminal charges for his article. The legal problems forced Lundy and Garrison to halt publication of the paper in early March. Later that month, Garrison went to court and was quickly tried by a jury. They found him guilty, and the judge sentenced him to either pay a fine, which Garrison could not afford, or to serve six months in jail.

On April 17, 1830, Garrison began serving his sentence. Fortunately for him, prison did not turn out to be such a bad experience. The warden did not consider Garrison a particularly dangerous inmate, so he allowed him to have visitors,

and he even invited Garrison to eat with him and his wife. Garrison used the time to write a number of letters. He joked in a letter to a friend that at least he did not have to pay rent. Garrison also used the time to pen an account of the trial. This vivid description of the injustice of the slave system soon helped end his time in jail. A wealthy merchant and philanthropist in New York City, Arthur Tappan, who was known to give money to antislavery causes, read Garrison's description of the trial. He then wrote to Lundy and offered to pay Garrison's fine to get him out of prison.

Tappan's generosity earned Garrison his freedom on June 5, but Lundy and Garrison agreed that it was best for them to continue their work separately. While Lundy planned to start up his paper again as a monthly publication, Garrison moved back to Boston to try to start a paper of his own.

He had no money, but he still did have his passion for the cause. Even more important, he believed that he was right, no matter what anyone else might say. In the fall of 1830, he wrote the following in a letter to a local paper:

I hold no fellowship with slave owners. I will not make a truce with them for even an hour. . . . They are dishonest and cruel, whether they know it or not, whether they believe it or not—and God, and the angels, and devils, and the universe know that they are without excuse.

At the time, Garrison might have been the only one who thought that he could do much of anything to end slavery. But he truly believed that with some persuasion other Americans would start to oppose slavery, too. When the new year arrived, Boston and the rest of the country would begin to find out just how dedicated and persistent Garrison could be.

Opposite page: An 1881 engraving of a ship loaded with slaves
(Courtesy of iStockphoto.com)

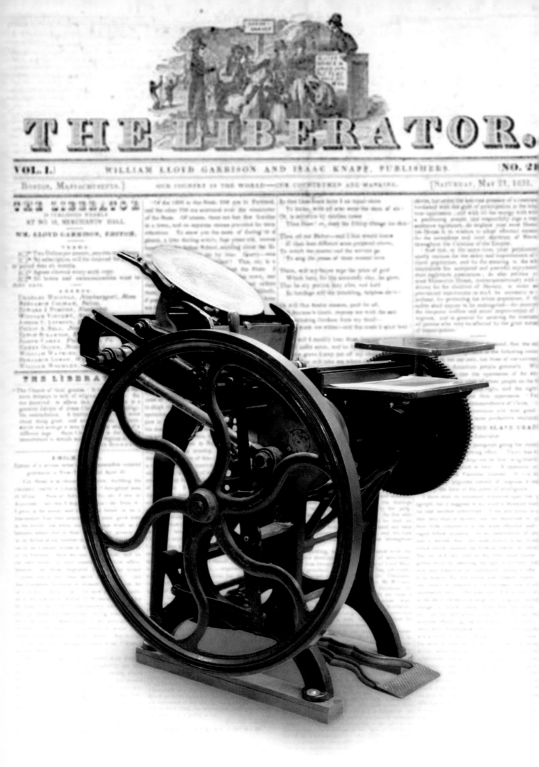

Chapter
3

The Liberator

When Garrison arrived back in Boston, his attempts to start an antislavery paper were met with indifference. It seemed that few people in the North gave much thought to the issue, and those who did often had an interest in allowing slavery to continue. Even worse, Garrison began to think that Northerners might be even more prejudiced than Southerners when it came to their feelings toward black Americans.

To most white Americans in both the North and South, slavery simply seemed to be a part of life. More than 2 million slaves were held as property by 1830, about twice as many as at the time of Garrison's birth. Most white Southerners did not own slaves, but even the poorest whites saw themselves as standing several rungs above blacks on the South's social ladder.

Slavery had not been a major political issue since 1820. In 1819, Missouri, which was then a territory, applied to be admitted as a state. This caused some tension among politicians, as the number of slave and free states had been balanced at eleven each, which meant that the Senate had an equal number of senators from each region. Northern politicians feared that allowing Missouri to enter the Union as a slave state would shift the balance of power to the South.

To try to satisfy both sides, Senator Henry Clay of Kentucky proposed a compromise: Missouri would be admitted as a slave state, but Maine would be admitted as a free state. The agreement also created a line at the southern border of Missouri; in the future, territories north of that line would be admitted as free states, and territories south of that line would be admitted as slave states. With the Missouri Compromise in place, slavery became a settled question, and politicians from all states tried to avoid talking about the issue as much as possible.

Most white Americans agreed that arguments about slavery should not disrupt the nation. But William Lloyd Garrison hoped to make a career out of disruption. While he searched for financial support for his paper, he also began giving lectures during which he attacked slavery. With his reputation for causing trouble, he had some difficulty finding places to speak. But in October 1830, he gave an address to a crowd of Bostonians, many of whom were wealthy and influential. One of those in the audience was Samuel May, a minister from Brooklyn, Connecticut. May was deeply impressed by Garrison's speech. He later recalled that hearing Garrison speak was so inspiring that he decided that night to dedicate himself to the fight against slavery. After the speech, May spoke with Garrison for hours about abolition and promised to help him in this cause.

With the encouragement of May and a gift of one hundred dollars from Arthur Tappan, twenty-five-year-old William

A manuscript Bill of Sale, dated October 10, 1807, for the sale at auction of the "Negro Boy Jacob" to Seth Griffith, the high bidder, for $80.50 in partial settlement of a money judgement against Prettyman Boyce, defendant, whose "property" Jacob had previously been. *(Courtesy of The Cooper Collection of U.S. Historical Documents)*

Lloyd Garrison finally started his paper. He convinced Isaac Knapp, a friend with whom he had worked at the *Newburyport Herald,* to work with him, and they soon found a room in an office building in central Boston that became both their workplace and their home. As the new year approached, Garrison worked hard to prepare the ambitious new paper, which he planned to call the *Liberator.*

On January 1, 1831, Garrison published his first issue. At the top of the page, in large black print, was the name of the paper. Just below that were the names of Garrison and Knapp. And below their names, printed in all capital letters, was the paper's motto: "OUR COUNTRY IS THE WORLD—OUR COUNTRYMEN ARE MANKIND."

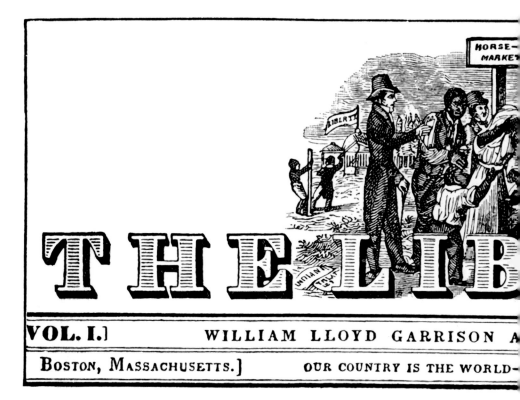

Garrison began his venture with an editorial in which he announced the purpose of the paper. He wrote that he would "lift up the standard of emancipation in the eyes of the nation." He also promised that the paper would stay out of political battles and try instead to get help from people of all parties. In his most famous line, Garrison declared that "I am in earnest— I will not equivocate—I will not excuse—I will not retreat a single inch—AND I WILL BE HEARD." That was a promise that Garrison had no trouble keeping.

Garrison published his paper every week for the next thirty-five years. That January, however, it looked as if the paper

ISAAC KNAPP, PUBLISHERS. [NO. 22.

R COUNTRYMEN ARE MANKIND. [SATURDAY, MAY 28, 1831.

might not even survive its first year. The newspaper business was fiercely competitive in the mid-nineteenth century, and many papers failed quickly. The fact that the *Liberator* focused on a subject that most white Americans usually ignored only made things harder. But one group that did care about the issue of slavery was the community of free blacks in the North. Before long, black Americans in the North accounted for about three-quarters of his subscriptions, and many more read the paper as it was passed from person to person. The money that came in from black subscribers kept the *Liberator* afloat in that first year.

Samuel May and other friends of Garrison also did what they could to raise subscriptions. At the end of February, he had ninety subscribers in Philadelphia and thirty in New York. By summer, Garrison had sold about five hundred subscriptions in all.

Garrison's editorials and articles on slavery occupied much of each issue, of course, but he also tried to give his paper a literary feel by including book reviews, a page of poems, and other similar works. As he had done at other papers, he often contributed a poem or two of his own.

Garrison and Knapp worked almost endlessly, particularly Garrison. The paper was not just a business venture for him, it was a calling. He continued to take on other work during the day to make a living, and then

A composing stone. Each week Garrison made up the type of the *Liberator*. (Courtesy of New York Public Library)

he would spend much of the night working on the *Liberator*. He worried that he did not have enough time to devote to the paper and that readers might not find it worthwhile. He complained in a letter to Samuel May that "the public imagine[s] that I have six days each week to cater for it, when, in fact, scarcely six hours are allotted to me, and these at midnight."

Although the paper took long hours and did not bring much financial reward, Garrison was at least being heard. That summer, he and Knapp published a collection of Garrison's speeches and sold out the entire first printing of one thousand copies. He was even being read in the South. Southern newspapers sometimes reprinted parts of Garrison's attacks on slavery and then included their own angry responses. Garrison received a number of letters from readers from the South. Often these letters included insults; some even threatened his life. By the end of the summer of 1831, events in Virginia would bring even sharper criticism from the South.

In August, a slave preacher in Virginia named Nat Turner planned and led a brutal and deadly slave rebellion. He and six other slaves murdered Turner's owner and his family and then continued to nearby houses, gathering more slaves and killing more whites as they went. Over the course of the two-day revolt, Turner's band of rebels killed fifty-seven whites in all, including women and children, before the revolt was put down by hundreds of white Southerners. Paranoid slaveholders and

A 1880 illustration depicting Nat Turner and fellow slaves gathering to plan a revolt. (Courtesy of New York Public Library)

other whites in the area ended up killing more than one hundred slaves in the aftermath of the rebellion, most of whom were not involved with Turner's actions. Turner managed to escape capture for two months, but he was eventually caught, tried, and executed.

Nat Turner's rebellion made news across the country. Garrison began receiving death threats from Southerners who angrily accused him of encouraging slaves to revolt. Papers throughout the South also blamed Garrison and called for him to be silenced. Even state legislatures in the South began to take action against Garrison. A town in South Carolina declared that any free black who subscribed to the *Liberator* would be fined. The city of Raleigh, North Carolina, indicted Garrison on charges of inciting slaves to rebel. In Georgia, the state legislature offered $5,000 to anyone who would arrest Garrison and bring him to the state for a trial.

Nat Turner and the other slaves who revolted brought much more attention to the editor of the *Liberator*. Garrison was suddenly famous. But the violence of the attacks by Turner posed a philosophical problem for Garrison. He opposed slavery and wanted it to end as quickly as possible, but he was also a pacifist—he opposed the use of any type of violence. He thought carefully about his response to the bloody events in Virginia. In an editorial published in early September, Garrison wrote that his prediction that slavery would lead to bloodshed had come true, but he also condemned the use of violence by the slaves. He warned that as long as slavery was allowed to continue, it was likely that there would be more incidents similar to Turner's rebellion in the future. In response to the accusations that he bore responsibility for encouraging slave revolts, he said that the slaves did not need him to give them a reason to rebel. The sufferings they endured at the hands of their owners was more than enough to inspire rebellions, he wrote. He was only surprised that there had not been more violence.

The furor over the slave rebellion eventually died down. The South became even more defensive about criticisms of slavery, and most Northerners continued to be unwilling to disturb the South by bringing up the issue. This indifference bothered Garrison, so he began to think about new ways to force people to pay attention. In the fall of 1831, Garrison, Samuel May, and several others who sympathized with the cause of antislavery formed an antislavery society. By mid-November, the group held its first meeting, but it did not go well. Those who attended could not agree whether to make immediate emancipation the goal of the society or to take a more gradual approach. Finally, after several more meetings, they agreed to adopt immediate emancipation as their objective, and the New England Anti-Slavery Society (NEAS) was born.

Arnold Buffum, a prominent merchant, was elected as the society's president, and Garrison was named the corresponding secretary. It soon became clear, though, that Garrison's energy and zeal would make him the dominant figure in the organization, whatever his title might be. Annual memberships to the NEAS were set at two dollars, and a lifetime membership could be purchased for fifteen dollars.

With the *Liberator* gaining more subscribers and the NEAS taking on some of the duties of antislavery agitation, Garrison finally had time to write a book about the colonization movement. This was something he had long hoped to do. In the summer of 1832, he finished and published the book, titled *Thoughts on African Colonization.* Garrison sharply criticized the American Colonization Society (ACS) and argued that the ACS was not really an antislavery society. Its goal was not to end slavery but to ensure the separation of blacks and whites. The book helped destroy the little support that the ACS still had, and it brought additional members to the New England Anti-Slavery Society.

Despite the growth of the antislavery movement, the end of slavery seemed as far away as ever in the United States. Garrison and other abolitionists looked to Great Britain for encouragement and inspiration. By 1833, it seemed that British abolitionists might be on the verge of convincing Parliament to abolish slavery in the West Indian colonies controlled by Great Britain. With the help of money raised by the New England Anti-Slavery Society, Garrison sailed for England in the spring of 1833 to meet these abolitionists.

Garrison arrived in Liverpool on May 23 after a three-week voyage across the Atlantic. He was the first person on board the ship to become seasick, he wrote in a letter, but otherwise the trip had been pleasant. Garrison then traveled to London, where he met many of the country's most prominent antislavery reformers. One British activist expressed his surprise upon

St. George's Hall, Liverpool, England, circa 1890s
(Courtesy of the Library of Congress)

meeting Garrison in person; he had expected Garrison to be black. Garrison's timing proved to be fortunate. While he was abroad, Parliament passed a bill that set August 1, 1838, as the date on which slavery would be abolished in the British West Indies, meaning that the 750,000 slaves held in those colonies would be free within five years. It was a thrilling experience for Garrison.

After being so warmly received in England, Garrison might have felt some reluctance when he boarded the ship to return to the United States. Immediately upon his return, he received a reminder of how much work was left to do. Newspapers in New York City had depicted Garrison as a traitor for criticizing the United States in his speeches in England, and angry mobs prepared to give him a rude welcome home. Fortunately for Garrison, friends helped him to safety when he arrived in New York. Still, it was not an easy time to be an American abolitionist. He and his fellow reformers remained a small and—as Garrison would soon find out—endangered minority.

Ledger and Jaynes buildings on Third Street in Philadelphia in the mid 1800s. (Courtesy of North Wind Picture Archives/Alamy)

Chapter
4

Courtship and Courting Danger

B y the fall of 1833, the New England Anti-Slavery Society was no longer alone in its efforts to bring slavery to an end. More than fifty other small, local groups had sprung up across the North. The movement still had few supporters, but it was growing. To take advantage of this growth, Garrison and Arthur Tappan helped lead an effort to create a national antislavery organization that would unite the small societies.

In December, Garrison, Tappan, and sixty other abolitionists met in Philadelphia and formed the American Anti-Slavery Society (AAS). Among the people who attended were John Greenleaf Whittier, the poet whose first poems had been published in Newburyport by Garrison; James Birney, a former slaveholder who had freed his slaves and become an abolitionist; and Theodore Weld, a young minister from Ohio.

The long days of meetings began at ten in the morning and did not stop until nightfall. By the end of three days, the abolitionists had agreed on a Declaration of Sentiments that presented the society's objectives. Garrison wrote the declaration himself, although changes were made after everyone read the document. There was one change, in particular, that Garrison did not like. He had written in one passage that anyone who held slaves was a "man-stealer." One of the other men in attendance objected that this was too strong a statement. As a compromise, the convention agreed to include a reference to a Bible verse to support the description of slaveholders as "man-stealers." Garrison objected to the change because he did not think it was necessary to use a reference to the Bible to prove that slavery was wrong. Everyone had the right to be free no matter what the Bible or any other book said, Garrison thought.

For the most part, however, the Declaration of Sentiments mirrored Garrison's usual attacks on slavery. Garrison wrote that the abolitionists were trying to put the ideals of the Declaration of Independence into action. He also said that the society would only support nonviolent means to end slavery. All the men in attendance signed the document, including the three African American members of the society. The most radical part of the society's objectives was the assertion that whites and blacks were equal and should be given the same rights and privileges. There were not many white Americans at the time who would have agreed. Another potential source of dispute was the role of women. Several women attended the meeting, but they were not allowed to sign the declaration. In a few years, the question of how involved women should be in the abolitionist movement would become a divisive issue.

The society chose Arthur Tappan as its president and named Garrison to the executive committee. There was some discussion about using the *Liberator* as the official paper of the organization, but in the end everyone agreed that it would be better to allow Garrison to continue to publish independently.

After the success of the meeting in Philadelphia, Garrison began to concentrate on a more personal matter. Earlier that year, he had met a young woman named Helen Benson. Garrison had already met Helen's brothers, Henry and George W. Benson, who were active in the abolitionist movement and were friends with Samuel May. The Benson brothers brought Helen with them to hear Garrison speak at a church in Providence, Rhode Island. They had been praising Garrison to Helen for months, so she was excited to have the chance to meet him. After Garrison's lecture, George invited Garrison to spend the weekend at the Benson family home in Brooklyn, Connecticut, which was about thirty miles from Providence.

Helen Garrison
(Courtesy of Library of Congress)

Garrison and Helen took to each other immediately. Garrison, despite his pale complexion and small build, could be impressive when he began to speak on the subject of slavery. But he also had a reputation among friends for his gentleness. People who knew him only from his speeches were often surprised upon meeting him in person to find that he was so soft-spoken. Helen was also quiet. She had brown hair, blue eyes, and a modest, kind demeanor. The two seemed to be a perfect match.

Garrison, however, left for England soon after meeting Helen. Due to his trip abroad and the excitement of the meetings in Philadelphia, he did not have time to pick up his courtship of Helen until early in 1834. On January 18, 1834, he wrote the first of many letters to Helen. He talked about the weather, mentioning the recent thaw, and then rambled for a bit about the differences in the seasons. Of course, he also discussed his favorite topic, abolitionism. He said that perhaps Helen could start an antislavery society in Providence.

The exchange of letters between men and women was not a matter to be taken lightly in the mid-nineteenth century. Helen did not want to seem too forward in her response, but she did like Garrison and wanted to encourage his attentions.

A nineteenth-century illustration of Boston, the capital of Massachusetts
(Courtesy of 19th era 2/Alamy)

She replied to him, saying that she did not think she was influential enough to start an antislavery group. The two continued to send each other letters over the next few months. In late February, Garrison visited Brooklyn again, and while he was there he decided that he wanted to marry Helen. He wrote in a letter soon after the visit asking her, "Have you any thing to give me *in the shape of a heart*, Helen?"

Garrison was overjoyed when she replied that she felt as strongly for him as he did for her. "Yes, my fears are dispelled," Garrison wrote to Helen, "my hopes are confirmed—and I can

shed delicious tears of joy!" Garrison wrote to Helen's parents to ask them for Helen's hand in marriage, and by April it was settled. Over the next few months, Garrison and Helen wrote dozens of letters to one another. "Do I think of you too often?" Garrison asked in one letter. "Do I devote too much time in writing to you? This I know—that our separation is truly painful to my heart; that you occupy my thoughts more than any other human being."

On September 4, 1834, Helen Benson and William Lloyd Garrison were married in Brooklyn by Samuel May. They soon moved to their new home, which consisted of several rooms rented in a house just outside Boston. They shared the house with Isaac Knapp and Knapp's sister. Before long, this space seemed too crowded, and the next spring they moved to a house in Boston's West End. By the summer of 1835, Helen was pregnant with their first child.

Garrison spent many years working closely with ambitious and strong-willed women involved in the abolitionist movement, but he had hoped to find a wife who would help him create a refuge in his home from the constant struggle to end slavery. "I did not marry her, expecting that she would assume a prominent station in the anti-slavery cause, but for domestic quietude and happiness," Garrison wrote to Helen's brother George. Helen proved to be a perfect match for him. As for Helen, by marrying Garrison she chose to leave the comforts of her middle-class home for a humbler and more precarious way of life. She knew it was likely that her husband's anti-slavery mission meant that he would always struggle to make enough money to support the family.

It did not take long for Helen to find out that money was not the only thing that she would have to worry about as the wife of the country's most famous abolitionist. The members of

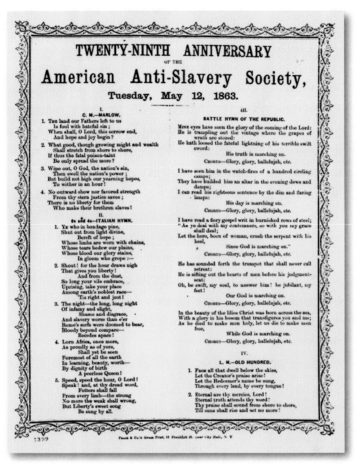

(Courtesy of the Library of Congress)

the American Anti-Slavery Society had kept their promise to increase their agitation against slavery, and many Americans were not happy about these activities. Over the months and years following the formation of the society, members formed local antislavery organizations across the North. Female members started women's antislavery societies in cities such as Boston, Philadelphia, and New York. In 1835, the AAS started a massive mailing campaign to send antislavery articles and leaflets to ministers and politicians in every state, especially in the South. Over the next two years, the society mailed more than a million documents.

Southerners became angry at the bombardment of anti-slavery literature through the mail. President Andrew Jackson, a Southerner himself, criticized the mailings and asked Congress to pass laws against using the mail to send antislavery documents. Even in the North, many newspapers continued to attack the abolitionists as dangerous radicals.

Garrison knew that his attacks on slavery could make him a target of mob violence. He mentioned in a letter to Helen's brother George Benson that there had been threats against his life made throughout the South and that most politicians seemed to be competing to be the most critical of the abolitionists. But, he said, these threats did not bother him. "My mind is full of peace," he wrote. If he were killed, it would only help put an end to slavery.

Criticism of abolitionists grew even louder in 1835 when British abolitionist George Thompson traveled to the United States to speak against slavery. Thompson and Garrison had become close friends during Garrison's trip to England. A women's organization, the Boston Female Anti-Slavery Society, invited Thompson to give a speech at one of its meetings in October. When newspapers in Boston learned of Thompson's scheduled speech, they began printing articles criticizing Thompson as an outsider. Many Americans still felt resentful toward the British because of the rivalry between the two countries since the American Revolution, so it was not hard to stir up the public's anger. The women's group had trouble at first finding a place to hold the meeting, because many owners refused to let them use their meeting halls. Finally, the women decided to use a room in their own Anti-Slavery Society offices.

As newspapers continued to fuel opposition to Thompson, rumors of death threats and mob attacks swept through Boston. To avoid putting his friend's life in danger, Garrison volunteered to take his place at the meeting. On the day of the scheduled speech, October 21, the editor of a local newspaper printed a flyer calling for Bostonians to prevent Thompson from speaking and offering one hundred dollars to the first person to try to do so. Thompson was not even in Boston on the afternoon of October 21, but the members of the angry crowd outside the building did not know that, and by this time it might not have made any difference.

Outside, the crowd was large and noisy. Inside, the women tried to continue with their agenda despite the commotion. Before long, the mayor arrived and told the women that he would ensure their safety if they would leave immediately— otherwise, they would be at the mercy of the mob. At first the women refused to leave, but eventually the mayor convinced them that their lives would be in great danger.

Garrison remained in the back of the building, and after the women left, the crowd began shouting for him to come out. He tried to escape out the back, but the mob spotted him and cornered him in the loft of a nearby shop. The unruly men forced him to descend a ladder to the street below. As he reached the ground and seemed to be at the mercy of his attackers, two men who had been part of the mob had an unexplained change of heart. Instead of taking him to be tarred and feathered, they carried him through the streets to City Hall and handed him over to the mayor and several constables.

Even then, the danger was not past. The mayor said that it would be best to take Garrison to the city jail, where he would be safe. Garrison slipped into a horse-drawn carriage while the crowd was distracted, and the driver managed to rush away before the mob could catch them. After a night in jail, Garrison made it home safely, and then he and Helen left the city to stay with Helen's parents in Brooklyn, Connecticut.

Garrison later joked about the close call, but it certainly frightened both him and Helen, who was pregnant at the time. The next day, instead of reporting that Garrison had been attacked by a mob, local newspapers said that Garrison had provoked a riot. The violence outraged both Garrison and other abolitionists, and Garrison remained angry at the mayor's inaction. After all, no one was ever arrested or charged with any crime. It was, said Garrison, "the most disgraceful event that has ever marred the character of Bostonians."

George Thompson was also shocked, and he expressed his outrage in a letter to Garrison written soon after the incident. "A mob in Boston!" Thompson wrote. "The birth-place of revolution—the Cradle of Liberty!" It would take another revolution, Thompson predicted, before slavery could be overthrown.

The riot did produce a few small victories for the abolitionist movement. A number of Boston residents were angered and scared by the mob violence, even if they had not been sympathetic to abolitionism. Some even converted to the cause, including Wendell Phillips, a wealthy and influential Bostonian who said that the attack on Garrison convinced him that the abolitionists must be right. Membership in the American Anti-Slavery Society doubled by the next spring. "New subscribers to the *Liberator* still continue to come in—not less than a dozen to-day," Garrison wrote to Helen. "Am much obliged to the mob."

Garrison had often written and spoken of his willingness to give his life to free the slaves, but he was happy to have escaped. He and Helen lived in Brooklyn for almost a year,

Wendell Phillips, William Lloyd Garrison, and George Thompson, antislavery advocates (*Courtesy of New York Public Library*)

although Garrison often returned to the city to publish the *Liberator*. The owner of the building where Garrison and Knapp worked decided to evict them, fearing that an attack on their office would be next. So when Garrison returned to the city on November 4, he and Knapp had to find new offices for their paper. Still, despite the distractions, they did not miss an issue.

The next few months provided some welcome peace to the Garrison family. On February 13, Helen gave birth to a son, George Thompson Garrison, named for the British abolitionist. Garrison wrote a poem for the occasion that he published in the *Liberator*. The birth of George helped distract Garrison from the difficulties of his antislavery career. Garrison would continue to work as hard as ever, but now he had a family to welcome him home after long days spent toiling at his paper.

Abolitionist Thomas Clarkson addresses a meeting of more than five hundred delegates, including a liberated slave from the Caribbean islands, at the 1840 convention of the British and Foreign Anti-Slavery Society, as depicted in this painting by Benjamin Robert Haydon.

Chapter
5

Dissension
in the Ranks

The violent attack on Garrison in Boston made abolitionists across the North more determined than ever to succeed. Members of small antislavery organizations held
gatherings to promote their cause. Abolitionists went door-to-
door in their towns and convinced thousands of Americans
to sign petitions that called for Congress to end slavery in the
nation's capital.

But success had its problems. The slow pace of change
frustrated some abolitionists, and they began to argue about
the best way to fight slavery. Some wanted to become more
involved in politics, but Garrison and others argued that it
would take a change in morality, not politics, to free the slaves.
Disagreements increased in the late 1830s, and before long
abolitionists started taking sides against one another in bitter
disputes over tactics, the role of women, and religion.

The violence in Boston in 1835 made it more difficult for antislavery groups to find places to hold meetings. Building owners did not want to see their property destroyed. In January 1836, Samuel May was turned down sixteen times in his search for a meetinghouse to hold the annual gathering of the Massachusetts Anti-Slavery Society. Still, the abolitionists kept working. Garrison attended meetings of state antislavery societies in Rhode Island and Vermont in 1836, and the AAS continued its mailing campaign.

The barrage of antislavery mail sent by the AAS did not free the slaves, but it certainly made the South angry. In Charleston, South Carolina, angry Southerners burned piles of mail that contained literature sent by the abolitionists, and some postmasters refused to deliver it. In response to these mailings and the antislavery petitions that the AAS continued to send to Congress, the House of Representatives decided in 1836 that it would no longer even consider antislavery petitions. This became known as the "gag rule." For some politicians, this still was not enough. John C. Calhoun, a respected senator from South Carolina, pushed for a law that would make it illegal to deliver mail that criticized slavery.

In Illinois in 1837, proslavery residents attacked an antislavery editor named Elijah Lovejoy. Mobs already had destroyed his printing press twice before, but this time they went even further, shooting and killing the editor. The murder reminded Garrison that he had been fortunate to escape with his life two years earlier.

The gag rule and the murder of Elijah Lovejoy helped convince Southerners that Congress would try to protect their right to own slaves, but it made many people in the North angry. Abolitionists began to argue that Southerners wanted to take away the rights of white Northerners, including the right to free speech and the right to petition Congress. In Boston, several thousand people gathered at Faneuil Hall to protest the killing of Lovejoy. Even though most Northerners still did not want to abolish slavery immediately, more of them began to think that, eventually, it would have to be brought to an end.

One Northerner who felt that way was William Ellery Channing, a well-known minister in Boston. In 1835, he wrote a short book to argue that slaves should gradually be freed, but only over a long period of time. Channing believed that it did more harm than good for abolitionists to argue so fiercely against slavery.

Channing's book infuriated Garrison. When Garrison started his campaign against slavery, he had hoped that ministers would be strong supporters of abolitionism. It had been quite a surprise to find that most of them, even in the North, were indifferent to slavery. Garrison responded in the *Liberator* to Channing's book by criticizing the clergy for this indifference and urging his readers to not accept the compromise of gradual emancipation.

Garrison's editorial was not well received by ministers, and the disagreement between Garrison and church leaders continued to escalate. In 1837, a group of ministers wrote in a short pamphlet that true Christians could not support the *Liberator* because of Garrison's criticisms of the clergy. Now Garrison was irate. His religious beliefs were an important part of his opposition to slavery, even if his religious practices were out of the ordinary. He had grown apart from traditional church services as he became more bitter that most ministers refused to oppose slavery. He and Helen gradually stopped attending church regularly, although religion remained a central part of their everyday lives. Garrison believed that members of the clergy who did not condemn slavery were hypocrites for preaching about morality while ignoring what Garrison considered the most immoral institution in the country.

This public dispute with the northern clergy was not the only issue on Garrison's mind. Even as the *Liberator* had become infamous across the nation, its future remained in doubt because of its precarious finances. Every year seemed to end with the paper in debt, and it was only with the help and donations of friends of the abolitionist movement that there was enough money to keep the paper going. Despite his years of long hours and hard work, Garrison still made only just enough to support his family, and that family continued to grow.

On January 21, 1838, Helen gave birth to their second son, whom they named William Garrison, Jr. "Willie," as they called him, looked just like his brother George. Later that year, the family moved to a new home, which they rented from an abolitionist named Amos Phelps for twenty-five dollars a month.

With the birth of Willie, the year was off to a promising start. But for the abolitionists, it was a difficult time. The large demonstration after the murder of Lovejoy and the growing membership of the AAS seemed to indicate that their efforts were working. In May, however, Garrison and other activists were reminded that there was still much opposition to overcome.

A number of abolitionists gathered in Philadelphia in the spring of 1838 to take part in the opening of a new building that was to be used for speeches and other public events. After two days in the city, however, the abolitionists found that much of the public in Philadelphia did not support the gathering of men and women and blacks and whites to speak out against slavery. A large crowd filled the hall on May 16,

A hand-colored woodcut of a nineteenth-century illustration of proslavery rioters burning the print shop of abolitionist Elijah Lovejoy in Alton, Illinois
(Courtesy of North Wind Picture Archives/Alamy)

and many more people filled the streets outside. As Garrison gave a speech, some members of the crowd forced their way into the building and began shouting. Outside, people in the mob threw bricks through the windows, disrupting the meeting. Still the abolitionists continued, and after several hours the mob had dispersed and Garrison and the others were able to leave without further trouble.

The next day, the mayor of Philadelphia asked the abolitionists to end their meeting early to avoid violence. They agreed to leave, but once the building was empty a crowd broke in and began destroying the hall. Before long the building was torched, and by the next day it had been reduced to ashes.

Later in May, back in Boston, Garrison took part in the annual meeting of the New England Anti-Slavery Society in Boston's Marlboro Chapel. This time it was the crowd inside the building that caused a disturbance.

The trouble started when the society passed a resolution that admitted men and women to the convention on an equal basis. Some of the more conservative members of the society did not think that women should be as active as men in leading the organization. These members, who were mostly ministers, became even more upset after one woman, outspoken abolitionist Abby Kelley, was elected to an important committee. When the ministers tried to force Kelley off the committee, the society took a vote on the issue and decided to allow Kelley to remain. The conservative ministers were so upset that a number of them left the meeting. They blamed Garrison for the trouble, saying that his belief in the equality of men and women and his unusual religious practices were distracting the society from the mission of abolitionism.

Other people were growing upset with Garrison's leadership of the abolitionist movement for different reasons.

Garrison had always tried to keep antislavery activism separate from politics. He believed that success in politics required too many compromises, and he was not willing to make any com- promises when it came to the battle to end slavery. In fact, Garrison did not even encourage people to vote. He believed that all the political parties were corrupt. In his eyes, it would do no good to support any party.

Abby Kelley

An abolitionist named James Birney strongly disagreed with Garrison. Birney once owned slaves him- self as a farmer in Alabama, but he had become convinced that slavery was wrong. After freeing his slaves, he joined the abolitionist movement. He spoke with many other slave- holders, and he knew how unlikely it was that many of them could be convinced to free their slaves. Criticism from the North only made them more stubborn, he thought. Unlike Garrison, Birney wanted to take political action against slav- ery. He thought that the abolitionists needed to elect antislav- ery politicians if they wanted to have any chance of freeing the slaves.

Garrison admired Birney's antislavery work at first. Birney started his own paper, the *Philanthropist,* and the two men exchanged copies of their publications. "I read *The Philanthropist* with eagerness, delight, and to great edification," Garrison wrote to Birney in the spring of 1836.

In the late 1830s, however, Birney helped lead an effort to move the abolitionists in a different direction, away from the moral arguments used by Garrison and toward more widespread use of political organization. Birney also agreed with the more conservative abolitionists who had walked out of the New England Anti-Slavery Society meeting—those who thought that Garrison had become too radical on the issue of women's rights. If the abolitionists were to get involved in politics, they would need to attract a wide range of Americans to their cause, and Birney and other conservatives worried that Garrison's extreme views would prevent moderate Northerners from supporting an antislavery party. Birney and about one hundred other abolitionists met in April 1840 to form an antislavery political party. The members of the new party, which they called the Liberty Party, nominated Birney to run for president in the fall elections.

The debate between the two sides of the abolitionist movement grew increasingly bitter. A showdown came in the spring of 1840, when abolitionists from across the North gathered in New York City for the annual meeting of the American Anti-Slavery Society. Francis Jackson, the president of the AAS, wrote in a letter printed in the *Liberator* shortly before the meeting that "It cannot be disguised—it should not be, if it could—that serious dissensions have arisen in our ranks, to the detriment of our cause." Birney and the political abolitionists had their new party, but Garrison still had many supporters who agreed that the movement should not adopt any official political position. A large crowd of Garrison's supporters from Boston traveled to New York for the meeting.

Once again, controversy erupted, with Abby Kelley at the center of it. Not long after the meeting began, she was nominated to be part of a business committee. The convention took a voice vote to determine whether she should be approved. A loud "yes!" was followed by a loud "no!" To settle the matter, those in favor of the nomination stood, those opposed remained seated, and a count was taken. By a vote of 571 to 451, the convention approved Kelley's nomination. There was such an uproar after the vote that the meeting was adjourned for the day.

Little had changed by the next day. In the morning, those who opposed the inclusion of a woman on a business committee walked out of the main hall and met in the basement of the building. They declared that the dispute was not just about Abby Kelley but about all of Garrison's radical ideas and his opposition to political involvement. That afternoon, Garrison's opponents formed a competing abolitionist group, the American and Foreign Anti-Slavery Society. Meanwhile, those who remained upstairs continued their meeting.

Garrison considered the convention a great victory for the American Anti-Slavery Society, because the organization had withstood the attempts of the political abolitionists to take over. He reported to Helen that the meeting was "a glorious triumph." Immediately, Garrison faced another challenge. British abolitionists planned to hold an international antislavery gathering in London in June. In order to make it to the conference, Garrison had to leave without returning home first. He missed Helen and his boys while in New York. Even worse, he knew that going on the trip might mean that he would miss an important occasion: Helen was pregnant again and due to give birth soon.

Garrison thought about skipping the trip to England altogether, but he worried that missing the convention would be a victory for the political abolitionists, who had already sent representatives to attend. Garrison did not want his allies in

England to think that they had taken control of the abolitionist movement within the United States, so he decided to go ahead with the trip. After Garrison made his decision, a fierce storm prevented his ship from leaving port, stranding him in New York City for several days. It was a miserable time for Garrison. He did not like observing the vast disparity in wealth that separated the city's well-to-do citizens from its poor, and he was bothered by the craze for making money that seemed to pervade the city.

Finally, on May 22, Garrison's ship left for England. Rough seas made the first few days unpleasant—he wrote to Helen that he was the first person on board to get seasick—but blue skies and warm temperatures welcomed him when he finally arrived on June 17. The conference had started the previous week, and his opponents had already scored a victory. Those in attendance at the meeting had voted not to admit the female abolitionists who would be attending from the United States as members; they would have to watch the proceedings from the gallery. When Garrison heard this news, he quickly decided that, if some of his fellow abolitionists were to be excluded just because they were women, then he would not take part, either. He and other friends, both men and women, sat together in the gallery and refused to participate. The decision caused quite a stir at the convention, and every time Garrison's name was mentioned by a speaker, the crowd erupted in cheers and clapping. Once again, Garrison had turned a potential defeat into victory.

After the convention ended, Garrison took the opportunity to tour parts of England and Scotland. He learned on July 2 that Helen had given birth to another son almost a month earlier, on June 4. Both he and Helen had hoped to add a daughter to their family, but they were still delighted to have a third son.

At first, Garrison thought about canceling the rest of his trip to return home immediately, but, not knowing when he might be able to return, he decided to continue to Scotland. He wrote to tell Helen that he would return in August and that he was happy to hear the news. "So! I am now the father of three boys," he wrote. "Why, it was just the other day that I was a babe myself. How all these things come to pass, I cannot tell."

Garrison (Courtesy of Pictorial Press Ltd/Alamy)

Wendell Phillips *(Courtesy of Library of Congress)*

Chapter
6

A Call for Disunion

Garrison arrived back in the United States in mid-August, but it was not until September that he and Helen finally settled on a name for their third son: Wendell Phillips Garrison. As with George, they chose to name Wendell after a close friend in the abolitionist movement. In 1835, Wendell Phillips had been inspired by the attack on Garrison in Boston to throw himself wholeheartedly into abolitionism. Unlike Garrison, Phillips came from a prominent and wealthy family, and he had received an excellent formal education, including a degree from Harvard. The two men's abilities and backgrounds complemented each other well.

It was not easy to put up with the ridicule and criticism that came with being an abolitionist, so the friendships Garrison developed were vital to his success. He relied on friends both to provide financial assistance when the *Liberator* seemed on the verge of going out of business and to keep up his spirits when it seemed that the slaveholders never could be beaten.

In the summer of 1841, Garrison encountered another man who soon became a good friend and a strong advocate for slaves. While attending an antislavery convention on the island of Nantucket, off the southern coast of Massachusetts, Garrison met an escaped slave named Frederick Douglass. Douglass had been born into slavery in Maryland in 1818, but he escaped in 1838 by borrowing the papers of a free black man and taking a train to the North. He worked odd jobs for a couple years, but he hoped to be able to help the millions of slaves still held in the South.

Douglass asked to speak at the gathering in Nantucket. Although he was nervous, he impressed the audience, which included Garrison. After Douglass finished, Garrison stood and asked the listeners if they would ever allow Douglass to be returned to slavery.

"No!" the audience shouted.

Douglass's words inspired Garrison. "I shall never forget his first speech at the convention," Garrison later wrote. "I think I never hated slavery so intensely as at that moment." Garrison asked Douglass to work for the American Anti-Slavery Society as a speaker. Douglass hesitated at first, unsure of his abilities, but he accepted after more encouragement from Garrison.

Douglass soon developed into an outstanding orator. One of his strengths was that he could speak firsthand about the horrors of slavery. But by choosing to speak out publicly, Douglass was putting himself in danger. Federal laws allowed slave owners to travel to the North to capture "fugitive" slaves who had escaped. If Douglass became well known, it was possible that his former master would hear about him and try to return him to slavery.

Frederick Douglass, 1879
(Courtesy of the National Archives
and Records Administration)

The threat that Douglass could be enslaved again provoked Garrison to talk about the issue of fugitive slaves. Northern states were required legally to assist slave owners in capturing fugitive slaves, which outraged Garrison and other abolitionists. In 1842, a ruling by the U.S. Supreme Court reinforced the rights of slave owners. The court declared that individual states could not restrict slave owners from capturing escaped slaves through the use of jury trials or other legal procedures. Even in the North, black Americans such as Frederick Douglass could never stop worrying about losing their freedom.

To Garrison, it seemed that the whole weight of the federal government supported slavery. He began arguing that there was no reason to remain a part of a country that would enforce slavery so strictly. It would be better, he thought, to break up the Union and separate from the South.

In the fall of 1842, an incident in Boston brought home the power of the fugitive slave law. James Gray, a slave owner from Virginia, requested that an escaped slave named George Latimer, who had been living in Boston, be returned to him. A judge in Boston put Latimer in Gray's custody and gave Gray ten days to prove his claim on Latimer. Abolitionists responded with a strong legal defense, and Bostonians crowded the streets to protest against Latimer's return to slavery. In mid-November, the sheriff released Latimer because he feared that a mob would break into the jail and free him by force. Gray then decided that it was not worth his time and effort to pursue the case any further, especially because it seemed unlikely that he could win.

Latimer had his freedom, and the abolitionists had an important victory. The confrontation soon inspired a petition drive. Abolitionists secured 65,000 signatures on a petition demanding that the state pass a personal liberty law to protect fugitive slaves in Massachusetts.

For Garrison, the victory in the Latimer case came in the middle of a busy and sometimes difficult period for his family. Helen and Lloyd welcomed their fourth son, whom they named Charles Follen Garrison, on September 9, 1842. But the next month, Garrison's brother died. James Garrison had returned unexpectedly in 1839, and for a time he lived with Lloyd's family. He tried to give up drinking but was never entirely successful, and he had trouble finding work. The death put a damper on the family's joy over the birth of Charles.

That winter, it seemed that everyone in the house was sick. All four children came down with the chicken pox, and after they recovered, all but Charles caught scarlet fever. Even Garrison had a severe case of scarlet fever.

Later in 1843, after everyone had finally recovered from their various illnesses, Garrison and Helen decided to take the family to western Massachusetts for the summer. Helen's parents had sold their farm in Connecticut a few years earlier and invested in a cooperative community, the Northampton Association of Education and Industry. The residents lived and worked together, creating a community in which members shared both common values and any profits that were made. Helen hoped to spend time with her sister and mother, and the rivers and mountains made it a peaceful place to spend a summer. But about a month after the Garrisons arrived, Helen broke her arm when the horse-drawn carriage she was riding in tipped over. At first her arm would not heal properly, but after a doctor reset the bone several painful weeks later, Helen began to improve.

When the family returned to Boston in November, Garrison threw himself back into his work. The months away seemed to have revitalized him. He soon needed all his energy, as the issue of slavery crept back into national politics.

Since the Missouri Compromise in 1820, most national politicians had done their best to avoid discussing slavery. But by 1844, the potential annexation of Texas had made it impossible to ignore the issue any longer. In 1833, Texas had declared its independence from Mexico after thousands of American settlers had moved to the territory. Before long, residents of Texas, as well as many southern politicians, were hoping that the United States would annex Texas to make it a part of the Union. Most northern politicians opposed annexation, so for years Congress put the issue aside.

In 1844, Texas became an important issue in the campaign for president. There were by this time twenty-six states. Thirteen were slave states and thirteen were free states, which meant that Congress had an equal number of senators from the

An 1840 engraving of the Boston waterfront near Fanueil Hall. (Courtesy of ClassicStock/Alamy)

North and South. But if Texas were admitted as a slave state, it would throw off that balance and give the South more power. Many in the South felt that they were under attack from the North and that the addition of more slave states could provide insurance against antislavery sentiment in the North.

As politicians began to talk seriously about annexing Texas, Garrison grew more disgusted with his country. That spring, he led an effort to convince other members of the American Anti-Slavery Society that the organization should officially adopt a policy of disunion, meaning that the members would prefer that the North break from the South rather than be forced to be part of a nation that allowed slavery to continue. It took a great deal of discussion, but finally Garrison prevailed. In May, Garrison printed an official statement in the *Liberator* announcing the new policy of the AAS. "Three millions of the American people are crushed under the American Union," it declared. "The government is their enemy—the government keeps them in chains!" From now on, the motto of the AAS would be "NO UNION WITH SLAVEHOLDERS!"

Not many Northerners were prepared to go as far as Garrison and the AAS, but a growing number of people were beginning to question why the North should have to help the South maintain slavery. A dozen northern congressmen who opposed the annexation of Texas declared that, if Texas did become part of the nation, the North would have no further duty to support the Union. Although Garrison's views were still extreme, his opposition to slavery no longer seemed quite so radical.

In the fall elections, Democrat James K. Polk defeated Henry Clay, the Whig candidate, in the race for president. Polk's election was a major victory for slaveholders in the South, but his election resulted in part from the success of the

James Knox Polk. The full-length portrait is an engraving by
John Sartain from an original 1845 painting by Thomas Sully, Jr.
(Courtesy of Library of Congress)

Liberty Party. As in 1840, James Birney ran for president on
the Liberty Party ticket. The Liberty Party received only about
7 percent of the overall vote, but in New York it won enough
votes that would otherwise have been cast for the Whigs that
Polk won the state. The Whigs complained that if not for the
Liberty Party, Clay might have won.

The presidential election mattered little to Garrison. He
continued to believe that politics could not end slavery; only
a change in the nation's moral values could do that. He spent

the end of 1844 and the first months of 1845 criticizing Polk for the impending annexation of Texas, the "greatest crime of his age," as Garrison described it. Soon after Polk's victory, Congress passed a resolution that cleared the way for Texas to become part of the Union. In March, the Senate admitted Texas as a territory. It was not yet a state, but it looked as if it would inevitably become one. Garrison and other abolitionists feared that the large territory might actually be broken into several states, giving the South even more political power. In the end, to maintain a balance between North and South, Congress decided to make Wisconsin a state at the same time that it admitted Texas to the Union.

The annexation of Texas showed that abolitionists still had a lot of work left to do, but 1845 also brought some good news. In June, Garrison's printing office published a short autobiography written by Frederick Douglass, titled *Narrative of the Life of Frederick Douglass, an American Slave, Written by Himself.* Garrison and Wendell Phillips both wrote short prefaces to the book, and Douglass's account of the harshness of slavery sold well. Readers bought more than 4,000 copies during the next several months and 30,000 copies during the next five years.

Douglass combined the eloquence of Garrison and Phillips with the detailed knowledge of life in the South that came from growing up as a slave. Like many other slaves, Douglass never knew for sure who his father was, although he suspected that it might be his master. His mother lived on a plantation twelve miles away, so Douglass rarely saw her and hardly knew her even by the time she died, when he was seven.

Slave owners often did not give their slaves enough to eat, and many would get only one pair of shoes and one set of clothes each year, which by the end of the year would be little more than rags. "In hottest summer and coldest winter, I was kept almost naked," Douglass wrote in his narrative. He described how he would steal a sack used to carry corn and use it as a blanket to try to stay warm. As for food, Douglass and the other slaves on his plantation ate mostly boiled cornmeal, and they had to fight with each other to try to get enough.

Fortunately for Douglass, he was sent to Baltimore at the age of seven to live with a relative of his owner. There he learned to read, and the more he read the more he longed to escape. When his owner sent him back to the plantation, Douglass began teaching other slaves to read, until several slaveholders found out and put an end to the lessons. By 1838, Douglass had returned to Baltimore, where he worked in a shipyard earning wages that he had to turn over to his owner.

That summer, Douglass made plans to escape. He borrowed money from Anna Murray, a free black woman living in Baltimore whom he would later marry. He also borrowed papers from a free black man. These papers proved that the man was free, and Douglass looked enough like the man that they hoped he would be able to use the papers to satisfy anyone who questioned him. On September 3, he boarded a train for New York, and within a matter of hours he had reached the North.

Being recaptured by his master worried Douglass, especially after he published his book. With the help of other abolitionists, Douglass raised enough money to go on a speaking tour in England. He left the United States in 1845 and did not return until 1847. Douglass was amazed at how warmly he was welcomed in England, particularly in comparison to the widespread racism he had experienced in the United States.

While Douglass traveled around England, war broke out in the United States. The territory that made up Texas had long been part of Mexico, and even after Congress admitted Texas as a state in December 1845, Mexico refused to recognize Texas's independence. Texas and Mexico also disagreed about where exactly the border should be between them. Texas claimed to control all the land as far south as the Rio Grande, but Mexico argued that it owned much of that territory.

President James K. Polk realized that this dispute might give the United States a chance to expand much farther to the west. In 1846, he offered to buy the disputed territory, as well as New Mexico and California, from Mexico. At the same time, he sent soldiers into Mexico in case the offer to buy the land was refused. Mexico rejected the offer from Polk and, in April, Mexican troops attacked the American soldiers. Before long, the two sides were at war.

In the South, slaveholders welcomed the war, hoping that it would result in the acquisition of more territory that would eventually become slave states. In the North, this possibility led many people, including some politicians, to oppose the war. In August, a representative from Pennsylvania named David Wilmot spoke up for those who did not want to see slavery spread.

When a bill to pay for the war came before Congress, Wilmot proposed an amendment that would outlaw slavery in any territory acquired from Mexico. Wilmot was certainly not an abolitionist, but he was one of a growing number of Northerners who opposed slavery because it hurt white workers, who could not compete with slave labor. He was also one of many northern Democrats who felt that their party had become too dominated by slaveholders.

Southerners were furious; they felt betrayed by the proposed amendment. The House of Representatives, in which Northerners outnumbered Southerners, approved the amendment. But the Senate, which was balanced between representatives from slave and free states, rejected it. Although it did not became law, Wilmot's proposed amendment raised tensions between the North and South. By 1847, the United States had won the war. The victory brought a huge stretch of land from Texas all the way to the Pacific Ocean under American control. But the war, with the help of David Wilmot and other northern congressmen, also put slavery at the center of national politics. The days when politicians could ignore the issue were coming to an end.

William Lloyd Garrison, left, and Wendell Phillips
(Courtesy of the Boston Athenaeum)

William Lloyd Garrison
(Courtesy of Lebrecht Music and Arts Photo Library/Alamy)

Chapter
7

The Consequences of Compromise

Garrison welcomed the increased attention the nation now paid to the spread of slavery, but as always he felt that the problem would not be solved through politics. Other abolitionists disagreed. These disputes could result in bitter divisions, even among the closest of friends.

In the summer of 1847, Garrison set out for a speaking tour of western Pennsylvania and Ohio with Frederick Douglass, who had recently returned from Great Britain. While Douglass was abroad, a group of British abolitionists had raised money to buy Douglass's freedom from his former owner in Maryland. The decision to allow them to do so was not easy for Douglass, but he felt that he could do more for the abolitionist cause if he did not have to worry about the possibility of capture. Garrison and Douglass decided to travel to Ohio, where Abby Kelley, her husband (Stephen Foster), and other abolitionists were successfully stirring up antislavery sentiment.

Douglass ran into trouble before he could give his first speech on the trip. He arrived at the train station in Philadelphia and took a seat in one of the cars. The railroad cars were not segregated, but a white man demanded that Douglass give up his seat. Douglass replied that he would be happy to do so if the man would just ask politely. This seemed to anger the man, who responded by physically throwing Douglass off the train.

That would not be the last resistance Douglass and Garrison came across. When Douglass stepped up to the podium to give a speech in Harrisburg, Pennsylvania, the crowd threw rotten eggs and firecrackers at him. A few days later in Pittsburgh, however, a more receptive audience cheered Douglass.

After a hectic schedule of travel and speaking, Garrison and Douglass arrived in Cleveland, Ohio, in early September. They expected to stay for just a few days before leaving for Buffalo, New York, but Garrison suddenly fell ill. He was too sick to continue the tour, so he stayed behind with friends in Cleveland while Douglass continued the trip. Garrison's condition worsened quickly, and at one point it seemed that he might be on his deathbed. Finally, Garrison started to recover, although he lost twenty pounds and had to spend more than three weeks confined to a bed.

Garrison felt hurt that Douglass had not tried to find out about his condition after continuing the tour. Even worse, when Garrison returned home he learned that Douglass had decided to start an antislavery paper of his own. The two men had discussed this possibility several times, but Garrison thought they had agreed that it would be more productive for Douglass to continue speaking, rather than to take the risk of going into the competitive newspaper business. Douglass, however, felt that if he were able to succeed, it would provide proof that black Americans were the intellectual equal of whites.

Many white Americans believed that blacks were not as intelligent as whites, and they used that belief as an excuse for slavery and racism. Douglass hoped that he could be living proof of the talents of black Americans. Unlike most white Americans, Garrison agreed with Douglass about the equality of blacks and whites, but he felt that it was a waste of Douglass's talents to spend his time running a paper. In the end, Douglass decided to proceed with his venture. He named the paper the *North Star* and began publication late in 1847. It was not a good decision, Garrison wrote to Helen.

Unfortunately for both Garrison and Douglass, they could not overcome their disagreement. Their close friendship ended.

Beneath the masthead of Frederick Douglass's newspaper the *North Star* is the paper's motto: Right is of No Sex—Truth is of No Color—God is the Father of Us All, And All We are Brethren. *(Courtesy of the Library of Congress)*

It was not the first time that Garrison had lost friends because of arguments about abolitionist strategies. The cause seemed so important that small misunderstandings could quickly escalate into major divisions. Since the split in 1840 between the American Anti-Slavery Society and the American and Foreign Anti-Slavery Society at the convention in New York City, the Liberty Party and the AFASA had become established as the political wing of the abolitionist movement, and Garrison and the AAS represented the nonpolitical abolitionists.

These disputes took a toll on Garrison, but fortunately his family provided a welcome break. In 1844, Helen and Lloyd finally welcomed the daughter they had been hoping for when Helen gave birth to Helen Frances Garrison, whom they soon nicknamed "Fanny." Two years later, in December 1846, another daughter was born, Elizabeth Pease Garrison, or "Lizzy." The Garrisons' last child, Francis Jackson Garrison, was born two years after Lizzy, in the fall of 1848.

Garrison loved having more children around the house, but it did make money tight. His salary was the same as it had been when he started the *Liberator,* but the number of people he supported was certainly not. The paper always seemed to be in financial trouble, especially when subscribers paid late.

Despite the constant financial troubles, the Garrisons always welcomed visitors. Friends and acquaintances frequently stopped by to visit, and the house became an informal gathering place for the abolitionist movement. Dinners were often occasions for rich conversations, which the entire family enjoyed. And when there were no guests to entertain, Garrison loved to spend time playing with his children. He would get down on the floor to take part in their games. Helen also indulged her children. She sometimes wrote in letters that she tried to be stricter but she had trouble punishing them. Garrison's gentleness with his family and his willingness to play with his children surprised some of his visitors, who expected him to be as stern in his personal life as he seemed to be when giving fiery speeches or writing fierce editorials.

Like many families in the nineteenth century, the Garrisons experienced their share of tragedy. Soon after Lizzy was born, Helen and Lloyd realized that her lungs were not functioning properly. She never seemed entirely healthy, and in the spring of 1848 she died from the flu. Lizzy's death devastated her parents. Helen had spent months caring for her child, and it would take several more months before she would begin to recover from the loss. The other children all came down with the flu at about the same time. "For a month past, our house has been little better than a hospital," Garrison wrote. "Dear Helen has had a severe time of it."

The next year, in April 1849, six-year-old Charles came down with a bad case of the flu. Helen wanted to call the doctor right away, but Garrison reassured her that it was not serious. After four days, however, Charles continued to worsen. Helen and Lloyd tried to treat Charles with a vapor bath, but they accidentally ended up badly scalding his side. "He became perfectly frantic," Garrison later wrote. "His screams were appalling." His parents finally brought in a doctor to examine him, but Charles's condition soon worsened. He died on April 8. The vapor bath did not contribute to Charles's death, but Helen and Lloyd blamed themselves nonetheless.

Two months later, Lloyd still felt overwhelmed by the tragedy. He wrote in a letter to a friend that the death of Charles was "a staggering blow, from the shock of which I find it very difficult to recover." Usually death did not bother him greatly,

Garrison wrote, as he believed it was a natural part of life, but "the loss of my dear boy has overwhelmed me with sadness."

Unfortunately, there was much work to be done. The acquisition of new territory during the Mexican War had raised the question of what to do with it—and whether slavery would be allowed. Once California applied for statehood under a constitution that would prohibit slavery, the issue could no longer be ignored. California would tip the balance of power to the free states if admitted, and Southerners worried that if the North had a majority in the Senate it eventually would try to outlaw slavery everywhere. South Carolina senator John C. Calhoun even warned that the South might secede if a compromise could not be found. This threat angered many Northerners, who felt that they had made enough concessions already to the slaveholders.

President Zachary Taylor, who had won the presidential race in 1848, declared that he thought that California should be admitted as a free state. New Mexico, he said, could eventually be admitted as a slave state to balance the two sides. But Taylor underestimated how strongly the South felt about the issue. Southern politicians reacted angrily to Taylor's proposal,

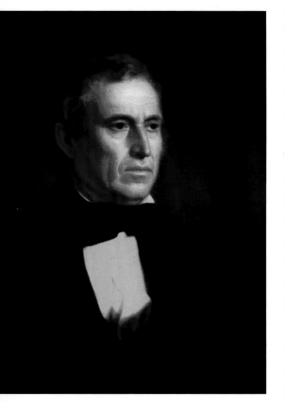

Zachary Taylor, as pictured in a 1850 portrait by John Vanderlyn

arguing that the North could not be given even a temporary edge in representation.

Henry Clay, a senator from Kentucky, stepped in to try to resolve the dispute. In January 1850, he proposed a compromise that he thought would appease both sides. California would be admitted as a free state, but when New Mexico and Utah were ready to apply for statehood, the residents of those territories would vote on whether to allow slavery. This approach, in which citizens would vote to settle the question of slavery, was known as popular sovereignty. The North would gain California as a free state, and the South would gain the possibility of opening vast areas of land for eventual admission as slave states. Clay's compromise also would end the slave trade in Washington, D.C., and, in return, the South would get a stronger fugitive slave law. A number of northern states had passed laws that made it harder for slave owners to claim and recover escaped slaves, so the South had argued for years that Congress should pass legislation that would counteract these laws.

President Taylor did not like the bill. He thought it gave away too much to the South. But after a Fourth of July celebration, he fell ill with terrible stomach pain. Five days later, he died. Vice President Millard Fillmore stepped into office, and he proved much more willing to support Clay's compromise.

Many congressmen from both the North and South opposed different parts of the bill, so it was impossible to pass the compromise at first. But Illinois senator Stephen Douglas broke the bill down into a number of separate bills and convinced enough senators to vote for each measure individually to pass the entire compromise. California became a free state, and the slave trade was abolished in the nation's capital.

Millard Fillmore
(Courtesy of Library of Congress)

Utah and New Mexico became territories without restrictions on slavery, and the South got its fugitive slave law. For the moment, it appeared that the compromise had avoided a larger conflict. Soon, though, it became clear that the controversy had just begun.

The personal liberty laws enacted by some states had given fugitive slaves some legal rights to contest the claims of slave owners. Some of the laws also had penalties for kidnapping that made it dangerous for slave owners to try to recapture runaway slaves. But the new fugitive slave law would require law enforcement officials to help slave owners claim their slaves, even in the North. It also made it a crime to help escaped slaves or to prevent their recapture, and it had severe penalties for anyone who broke this law. As for the runaway slaves, they would have no right to a trial by jury, and they could not even testify at the hearing. The claim would be decided by a federal commissioner. Commissioners who heard the arguments of slave owners would be paid ten dollars if they upheld the claim and only five dollars if they denied the claim. It seemed that the government was clearly on the side of slavery.

It did not take long for slave owners to test the new law. In September, a slave owner from Baltimore claimed that a black man in New York City was a slave of his who had escaped three years earlier. The federal commissioner who heard the case ruled that the man should be returned to Baltimore. In February 1851, a black man in Indiana was returned to the South after a slave owner claimed that he had run away nineteen years earlier.

The new law infuriated Garrison, of course. But what was surprising, even to Garrison and other abolitionists, was how many Northerners were angry about the law. By the end of

1850, nineteen escaped slaves had already been returned to slave owners from the South. Garrison used accounts of these cases in his paper to dramatize the horror of slavery and the immorality of slave owners. He asked his readers to imagine how they would feel if they had escaped from slavery only to be captured suddenly and returned to the South.

In Boston, the first confrontation over the law came in October 1850 when two white men from Georgia arrived intending to return two escaped slaves to their former masters. The runaway slaves, Ellen and William Craft, had run away from Georgia two years earlier and become popular speakers in Boston. A group of antislavery men who called themselves the Vigilance Committee helped the Crafts hide, and dozens of abolitionists followed the slave hunters wherever they went around the city to try to slow their progress. After a frustrating week in Boston, the two slave hunters gave up and returned to Georgia. To ensure that the Crafts would remain safe, local abolitionists raised enough money to send them on a trip to England.

An even more dramatic confrontation came in February 1851. Federal marshals arrested an escaped slave named Frederick Jenkins at the request of a slave owner from Virginia. Abolitionist lawyers rushed to the courthouse to try to prevent Jenkins from being returned to the South, and a large crowd gathered outside. Suddenly, a group of free black men burst through the doors of the courthouse and freed Jenkins, quickly sending him on his way to Canada.

Boston's abolitionists seemed to have defeated the slaveholders this time, but the victory would not last. The South reacted angrily to the freeing of Jenkins and demanded that those involved be punished. President Fillmore agreed, and he pressured Boston's leaders to prosecute the men who had helped Jenkins. The district attorney in Boston indicted eight men, but juries acquitted all of them.

When the next opportunity came for Boston's officials to enforce the fugitive slave law, they were ready. In April, officers arrested an escaped slave named Thomas Sims. Officials held him in a courtroom surrounded by policemen, chains, and ropes. No one other than the attorneys and commissioners involved in the case was allowed in the court. After a week of hearings, the commissioner ruled that Sims should be given over to his former owner. At four in the morning on April 12, three hundred law officers took Sims to the ship that would return him to the South and slavery.

Over the next few years, the fugitive slave law continued to cause controversy across the North, but in most cases it was enforced. Few cases came up in Boston, partly because runaway slaves left the city for places where they could feel safer. From the enactment of the law to the end of the 1850s, more than three hundred black men and women were returned to slavery, and only eleven were declared free by the commissioners hearing the cases.

The success of the law in returning escaped slaves brought more Northerners to the side of the antislavery activists. By the early 1850s, Garrison and the American Anti-Slavery Society no longer seemed so radical, although still most white Americans in the North did not yet believe that immediate emancipation of slaves was necessary.

The fugitive slave law helped inspire one northern white woman to bring slavery to the country's attention in a new and captivating way. In 1852, Harriet Beecher Stowe, the daughter of a prominent minister, published *Uncle Tom's Cabin,* a novel

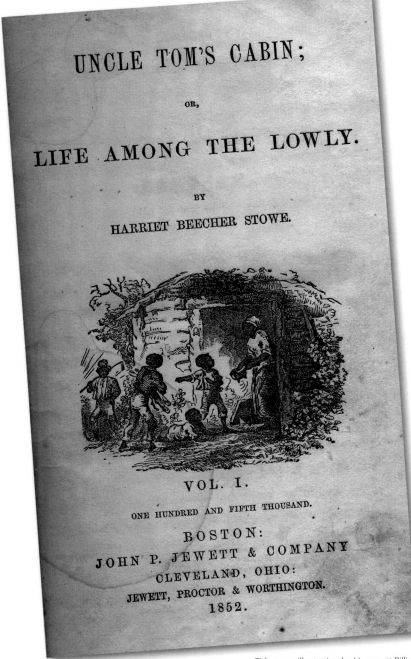

Title-page illustration by Hammatt Billings from *Uncle Tom's Cabin*, showing the characters Chloe, Mose, Pete, Baby, and Tom

about the lives of several slaves and the dangers they faced from their owners. The novel revealed to northern readers the harsh conditions of plantation life and the harm that slavery did to both black and white families. *Uncle Tom's Cabin* quickly became a sensation. It sold 10,000 copies in its first week and 300,000 by the end of the year. Stowe had spent little time in the South herself, but she used narratives written by slaves as the basis for much of her book.

Garrison loved the book and praised it for bringing to life the drama of slavery. Stowe and Garrison met not long after Stowe published her book, and the two became friends and allies in the abolitionist movement. Garrison knew that being involved in the abolitionist movement could be hard on friendships, but he also often found that commitment to this cause could bind people closely together.

U. S. Capitol, 1846. *(Courtesy of Library of Congress)*

94

Chapter
8

Lighting the Match

Despite all the uproar caused by the fugitive slave law and Stowe's book, both the Democrats and the Whigs tried to keep the issue of slavery out of the 1852 presidential election. The Whigs nominated Winfield Scott, a general in the Mexican War, and the Democrats nominated Franklin Pierce, also a veteran of the war. Pierce was from New Hampshire, which appealed to northern Democrats, but he also supported slavery and had no intention of questioning the rights of slaveholders, which appealed to Democrats in the South. With this broad base of support, Pierce defeated Scott for the presidency. This was the last time that the nation's politicians managed to keep the debate over slavery from dominating political discussions.

Garrison had spent much of the election year traveling across the Northeast and Midwest to speak at antislavery conventions. With the help of railroads, he made his way across the country much more quickly than he had at the start of his abolitionist career. An even more important change was that he now faced large, welcoming audiences at his speeches instead of angry mobs. The battle was far from over, but Garrison and his fellow abolitionists certainly had helped change the North's attitude toward slavery. White Southerners still thought of the antislavery movement as a group of extremists, but as they soon would find out, it was no longer just radicals who opposed allowing slavery to spread.

Franklin Pierce
(Courtesy of Library of Congress)

Although he was a Northerner, President Pierce agreed with many southern politicians that the country should continue to expand. Pierce hoped to obtain new markets to sell American goods, and southern planters wanted to gain more land that could be used to grow cotton with slave labor. In 1854, Pierce offered to buy the island of Cuba from Spain. Cuba lies just ninety miles to the south of Florida, and in the nineteenth century it was a rich sugar-producing colony that allowed slavery. White Southerners had long hoped to make Cuba part of the United States, but Spain never had been willing to sell. When Spain again rejected the offer by Pierce, three American ambassadors meeting in Belgium sent a confidential note to Pierce arguing that if Spain would not sell the island, then the United States should simply take it by force.

When the note became public, abolitionists and northern politicians charged that it was just another attempt by Southerners to gain more land for slavery.

Pierce gave up on acquiring Cuba after this incident, but before long another controversy arose about land in the West. In the nation's capital, most politicians had hoped that the Compromise of 1850 would settle the issue of slavery for years to come. But by 1854, it was clear that they had been too optimistic.

Lawmakers in the large territory of Nebraska, which sat to the west of Missouri and Iowa, hoped that Nebraska would soon be admitted as a state. As in 1850, the North and South argued over how to proceed. Senator Stephen Douglas, who had played a key role in passing the Compromise of 1850, proposed that the area be split into two territories, Nebraska and Kansas, and that the residents of each territory vote themselves on whether to allow slavery. According to the Missouri Compromise, which had been passed in 1820, slavery could not spread this far to the north, so Douglas's proposal would overturn that agreement. President Pierce endorsed Douglas's bill. In the spring of 1854, Congress passed the bill. Kansas and Nebraska would become separate territories and the question of slavery would be decided by the residents. It seemed likely that Nebraska, the more northern of the two territories, would outlaw slavery, whereas Kansas, which had a climate and soil similar to Missouri's, would allow it.

In the North, the repeal of the Missouri Compromise outraged many citizens. Rumors that southern slaveholders were conspiring to extend slavery across the entire country spread quickly, and resentment toward the "Slave Power" continued to grow. In mid-February, Garrison denounced the Kansas-Nebraska Act to a large audience in New York City. That such a crowd would attend an antislavery speech in New York City, where not long before abolitionists were treated as traitors, showed how much had changed in the North. Even Garrison was surprised at how warmly the crowd greeted him: "My language was strong, and my accusations of men and things, religion and politics, were very cutting; but, strange to say, not a single hiss or note of disapprobation was heard from beginning to end." In fact, Garrison wrote to Helen, "some of my strongest expressions were the most loudly applauded." After the speech, the *New York Times* requested a copy, which it printed the next day.

Not long after Congress passed the Kansas-Nebraska Act, Boston witnessed another dramatic confrontation over the fugitive slave law. On May 24, federal marshals arrested a runaway slave named Anthony Burns at the request of his former owner. The authorities held Burns in jail during a weeklong trial. President Pierce sent soldiers to Boston to prevent any disturbance and to ensure that sympathetic Bostonians could not free the escaped slave. It seemed to the residents of Boston that their city had been seized by the Slave Power. Protestors crowded into the streets to show their disapproval, but after the ruling went against Burns, soldiers escorted him to a ship that would return him to slavery.

The capture and return to slavery of Anthony Burns outraged Garrison and his fellow abolitionists in Massachusetts. Every year on the Fourth of July, the Massachusetts Anti-Slavery Society held a picnic. This year, to protest the incident, the Massachusetts Anti-Slavery Society decided that the picnic would be a day of public mourning. The contrast between the ideals of liberty and justice and the reality of slavery seemed more dire than ever for the six hundred or so abolitionists who

An 1856 map showing free and slave states, statistics for each of the states from the 1850 census, the results of the 1852 presidential election, congressional representation by state, and the number of slaves held by owners. The map is also embellished with portraits of John C. Frémont and William L. Dayton, the 1856 presidential and vice presidential candidates of the newly organized Republican Party, which advocated an anti-slavery platform *(Courtesy of Library of Congress)*

attended the picnic. The gathering turned out to be the scene of one of Garrison's most memorable speeches.

Garrison spoke on a platform that stood in front of an upside-down American flag. The Constitution, he said, "was formed at the expense of human liberty." Unlike some abolitionists, he believed that the Constitution was a proslavery document: "It is absurd, it is false, it is an insult to the common sense of mankind, to pretend that the Constitution was intended to embrace the entire population of the country."

The Founding Fathers had not cared about the condition of slaves, he declared. "The truth is, our fathers were intent on securing liberty to themselves." But it was Garrison's actions, not his words, that made his speech so unforgettable. He took a copy of the Constitution and lit it with a match, holding it as it burned.

Most white Northerners might not have been willing to go that far, but they were unhappy with the outcome of the debate over Nebraska. They took out their anger on politicians in the fall elections, and the result was a change in the nation's political parties. The Whig Party collapsed, as southern Whigs defected to the Democratic Party and many northern Whigs left the party for a new party, the Republican Party, which took a stronger stance against the spread of slavery. The Republicans did not intend to end slavery in the South, where it already existed, but they did oppose allowing it to extend into new states. Many Republicans feared that if slavery did spread, it would make it impossible for white workers to find jobs, as employers might choose to go with slave labor rather than pay for free laborers. Other Republicans were businessmen who wanted to encourage manufacturing and believed that slavery stunted the growth of the country.

Over the next two years, violent conflict erupted in Kansas as antislavery and proslavery residents vied for control of the territorial government. Settlers from nearby states even rushed in to try to take part in elections. The South had an edge in sending settlers, as Missouri bordered Kansas. To try to counter the South's advantage in geography, many Northerners raised money for clothing, food, and even guns to send to antislavery settlers in the territories, hoping that they could help swing the territory to the antislavery side before it was admitted as a state.

Missourians poured across the border to vote in the first elections, hoping to swing the territorial legislature to the proslavery side. But by 1855, antislavery settlers outnumbered proslavery settlers, and they set up their own territorial government. A proslavery government in the town of Lecompton was the official territorial government, but antislavery settlers had their own representatives form a competing government in the town of Topeka. It did not take long for the dispute to turn bloody, as the two sides vied for control of the territory. In 1856, hundreds of proslavery settlers attacked the town of Lawrence, which was controlled by antislavery Kansans. In response, an abolitionist named John Brown led an attack that killed five proslavery settlers. The violence escalated, and the skirmishes between the two sides eventually took the lives of about two hundred settlers.

Garrison did not want to see Kansas become a slave state, but he found it difficult to support the antislavery settlers. He opposed the use of violence and was surprised that so many other abolitionists seemed willing to condone the fighting in Kansas. He admired the courage of the antislavery settlers, but he maintained that the use of violence was not justified. "Is it not plain," he wrote in the *Liberator,* "that the

Abolitionist John Brown

cure for all this is to be found in a recognition of the sacred-ness of human life?"

Of course, as much as Garrison disliked the use of violence by those who opposed slavery, he was even more critical of the proslavery side, and he was not alone. In 1856, a prominent senator from Massachusetts, Charles Sumner, denounced the influence of southern slaveholders in Kansas. Sumner gave a speech to the Senate about what he called "the crime against Kansas." Sumner singled out a few senators in particular for their support of slavery, including Andrew Butler, a senator from South Carolina. After the speech, a congressman named Preston Brooks, who was related to Butler, viciously attacked Sumner with a cane, nearly beating him to death.

The attack upset Northerners, but what surprised them even more than the beating itself was the reaction in the South, where Brooks became a hero. Southerners sent Brooks new canes to replace the one he had broken while beating Sumner, and newspapers celebrated his defense of the South. That fall, voters in Massachusetts reelected Sumner to the Senate, even though he was still recovering from his injuries. Sumner was unable to return to Congress until 1860 due to his injuries. Until then, his seat remained empty. It was a constant reminder to other senators of the growing divide between North and South.

Massachusetts was not the only place where slavery was the key issue of the 1856 elections. Democrats in the South nominated James Buchanan for president. They were confident that he would protect their rights and allow slavery to expand. In the North, the growing Republican Party took advantage of the anger over the events in Kansas. They nominated John Frémont for president. Frémont was not an abolitionist, but he was a "free-soiler." He believed that slavery hurt white workers, but, unlike the abolitionists, he did not believe that slavery was necessarily wrong. Still, the nomination showed that the Republicans had a different approach to politics than the Whig Party, which had never taken a strong stance against the spread of slavery. A third party, the American Party, tried to win voters with its anti-immigration platform.

James Buchanan *(Courtesy of Library of Congress)*

With strong support in the South, Buchanan won the election. He gained a majority in every southern state except Maryland, and he also won five free states. Overall in the North, Frémont won more votes than either Buchanan or Millard Fillmore, showing how far the Republican Party had come in just a few years of existence. The Republicans, however, had virtually no support in the South. To win a presidential election, they would have to take almost every free state. But if that happened, there was a risk that the Union would completely collapse.

For perhaps the first time in his career as an abolitionist, Garrison chose not to condemn all political parties. He still felt that change would not come about through the political process, but he did think that the Republican Party had promise as an antislavery party, and he was encouraged by its strong showing. Other abolitionists, such as Abby Kelley and Stephen Foster, took a harsher stance toward the Republicans. Garrison was no longer the most radical abolitionist around.

Not long after the election, the Supreme Court issued a ruling that reinforced Garrison's belief that the government was entirely on the side of the slaveholders. The case involved a man named Dred Scott, a slave from Missouri who had lived with his master for several years in territories that were not yet states. Scott argued that his time in the territories had made him free, because slavery was not officially recognized there. The case made its way to the Supreme Court, and in March 1857 the court ruled against Scott. Chief Justice Roger Taney concluded that Congress had no right to prohibit slavery in the territories. Even worse for Scott, Taney wrote that black Americans had no constitutional rights—no black person could be an American citizen.

The Supreme Court's ruling seemed to open the way for all the territories to become slave states. According to the court, slavery could not be prohibited in any territory. It also apparently took away all the rights of free blacks, even those who lived in the North. Garrison was furious, of course, and this time he was not alone. Newspapers across the North condemned the decision. But Southerners celebrated the ruling as a vindication of the rights of slaveholders. The divide between North and South continued to widen.

Garrison continued to believe that the North should dissolve the Union and break apart from the South. If the North did this, he thought, it would make it harder for the South to maintain slavery. The South would no longer be able to force

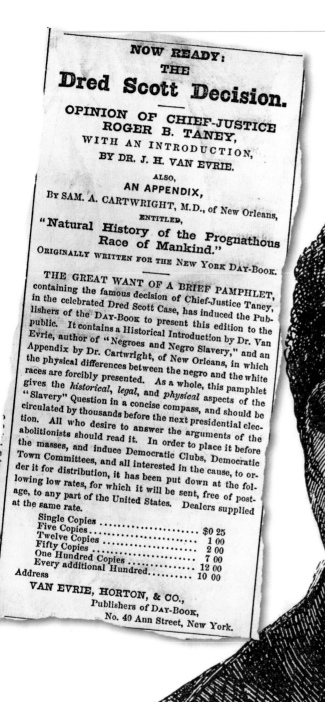

NOW READY:
THE
Dred Scott Decision.

OPINION OF CHIEF-JUSTICE ROGER B. TANEY,
WITH AN INTRODUCTION,
BY DR. J. H. VAN EVRIE.

ALSO,
AN APPENDIX,
By SAM. A. CARTWRIGHT, M.D., of New Orleans,
ENTITLED,
"Natural History of the Prognathous Race of Mankind."
ORIGINALLY WRITTEN FOR THE NEW YORK DAY-BOOK.

THE GREAT WANT OF A BRIEF PAMPHLET, containing the famous decision of Chief-Justice Taney, in the celebrated Dred Scott Case, has induced the Publishers of the DAY-BOOK to present this edition to the public. It contains a Historical Introduction by Dr. Van Evrie, author of "Negroes and Negro Slavery," and an Appendix by Dr. Cartwright, of New Orleans, in which the physical differences between the negro and the white races are forcibly presented. As a whole, this pamphlet gives the *historical, legal,* and *physical* aspects of the "Slavery" Question in a concise compass, and should be circulated by thousands before the next presidential election. All who desire to answer the arguments of the abolitionists should read it. In order to place it before the masses, and induce Democratic Clubs, Democratic Town Committees, and all interested in the cause, to order it for distribution, it has been put down at the following low rates, for which it will be sent, free of postage, to any part of the United States. Dealers supplied at the same rate.

Single Copies	$0 25
Five Copies	1 00
Twelve Copies	2 00
Fifty Copies	7 00
One Hundred Copies	12 00
Every additional Hundred	10 00

Address
VAN EVRIE, HORTON, & CO.,
Publishers of DAY-BOOK,
No. 40 Ann Street, New York.

Wood engraving of Dred Scott in *Century Magazine*, 1887 *(Courtesy of the Library of Congress)*

northern states to return runaway slaves, and the South would no longer have the manufacturing power of the North to help sustain its economy. In January 1857, Garrison and a number of other abolitionists in Massachusetts held a State Disunion Convention in Worcester. That summer, after the *Dred Scott* decision, Garrison, Wendell Phillips, and several other activists organized a larger convention to address the issue again. In an open letter asking people to attend this convention, the organizers declared, "For all our efforts, there is not yet an inch of truly Free Soil in the nation."

By now Garrison had passed his fiftieth birthday, and finally his life seemed a bit more secure. Friends of the Garrisons had raised several thousand dollars, which they used to buy the Garrisons their own home in Boston, not far from Boston Common. The children began to leave home to pursue their own careers. George worked off and on at the *Liberator,* but he always felt uncomfortable when he had to work too closely to his father. He yearned to strike out on his own rather than continue his father's work. In the spring of 1857, he left Boston for Minnesota, where he worked in a factory for some time before taking a job with a newspaper. His parents wrote him so many letters that George warned them that he could not possibly reply to each one, especially as he did not really enjoying writing letters very much.

Before long, George was on the move again, this time to Kansas, where the recent discovery of gold had inspired many Americans to try their luck there. He did not strike it rich, but he did find work with a newspaper. Back in Boston, his family missed him and waited for him to return home, but George felt that if he returned, he would always have to live up to the expectations of his famous father. Unfortunately for George, it was not easy to make enough money to get by, and the next spring he boarded a train back to Boston.

Willie, the second-oldest Garrison child, was also out on his own. Like George, Willie was not a great student, so he went to work with a shoemaker in 1855 to learn how to run a business. After a few years, he moved on to a bank in Lynn, Massachusetts.

Lloyd's third son, Wendell Phillips Garrison, was the family's academic star. Wendy, as they all called him, finished high school about the time George returned from the West. He had attended a prestigious public school, Boston Latin, where he graduated second in his class. With some financial help from his namesake, Wendell Phillips, Wendy then enrolled at Harvard College. Meanwhile, the younger children, Fanny and Frank, remained at home with their parents. Frank eventually attended Boston Latin, although he did not enjoy school quite as much as his older brother did.

Garrison enjoyed having his family close to him, so he was happy when George returned from Kansas. Within a few years, however, his oldest son left home again. This time, it was to join the Union Army.

A color print, circa 1887, depicting the Battle of Gettysburg, in Pennsylvania. The battle took place July 1 to July 3, 1863. It resulted in more casualties than any other battle in the war and is often described as a turning point in the conflict. Union Major General George Meade's Army of the Potomac defeated attacks by Confederate General Robert E. Lee's Army of North Virginia, ending Lee's invasion of the North. *(Courtesy of Archive Images/Alamy)*

Chapter
9

War!

In 1857, Garrison met John Brown, the abolitionist from Kansas who had been involved in the violent battles between proslavery and antislavery settlers. Brown was in Boston trying to raise money to train antislavery men in Kansas to fight against the proslavery side. Garrison did not condone such violence, and he had little money as it was, so it is unlikely that he contributed to Brown's fundraising efforts. But other Northerners reacted more enthusiastically to Brown's mission. There were rumors that Brown had been involved in the murder of five proslavery settlers in Kansas not long before. Though Brown denied the charges, it was later shown that he not only had participated in the raid but actually had led it.

Like Garrison, Brown felt passionately that slavery was immoral. But unlike Garrison, Brown had no qualms about using violence in his antislavery efforts. Brown had little patience for the long meetings held by abolitionist groups. It was action, not talk, that was needed, he thought.

On October 17, 1859, Brown showed that he believed what he said. He led a small party of twenty armed men into northern Virginia in an attempt to start a slave revolt. Garrison and Wendell Phillips were together when they first heard the news that there had been an attack in Virginia, and both immediately thought of Brown. Brown's party tried to seize a federal arms depot at Harper's Ferry, and they planned to distribute weapons to slaves. They hoped that their raid would inspire slaves to flee their owners. Instead, federal troops quickly ended the poorly planned attack, taking Brown prisoner and killing a number of his men in the process. Within weeks, Brown was tried, found guilty, and sentenced to death.

Many Northerners, including Garrison, were puzzled by Brown's actions. "Upon the face of it, his raid into Virginia looks utterly lacking in common sense," Garrison commented. Surely Brown could not have thought that he would succeed. Despite these reservations, many Northerners considered Brown a hero. Before being executed, Brown had the chance to give one final speech. His words became famous in the North, where printers republished his speech in newspapers and pamphlets: "Now, if it is deemed necessary that I should forfeit my life for the furtherance of the ends of justice, and mingle my blood further with the blood of my children and with the blood of millions in this slave country whose rights are disregarded by wicked, cruel, and unjust enactments, I submit; so let it be done!"

On December 2, the day the state of Virginia hanged John Brown, church bells rang in the North and speakers pronounced Brown a hero for his sacrifice. Garrison gave a speech celebrating Brown's intentions, even though Garrison did not condone the use of force. Brown's execution was expected, but for Southerners the widespread praise of Brown was not. They saw Brown as a murderer and a criminal, not as a hero.

Brown had not freed a single slave, but he did help make a split between North and South more likely. With war on the horizon, the country held national elections. The Republican Party continued to gain strength. The growing tensions between the regions finally resulted in the division of the Democratic Party along sectional lines. This meant that Republicans now had a good chance of winning the 1860 presidential election.

About a year before John Brown ignited the country with his brash actions, a man from Illinois named William Herndon had traveled to Boston to meet Garrison and other abolitionist leaders. Herndon was the law partner of a Republican politician named Abraham Lincoln, and he wanted to convince Garrison to support Lincoln for president. Herndon did not want Garrison to campaign publicly for Lincoln, because Garrison was still considered so radical that his endorsement might actually weaken Lincoln's campaign. Instead, Herndon asked Garrison to continue with his criticisms of both Democrats and Republicans, but to recognize that there was a difference between the proslavery Democrats and Lincoln, even if Lincoln could not come out against slavery as strongly as Garrison might like.

In 1860, the Republican Party nominated Lincoln for president. The party hoped that Lincoln would gain the support of both abolitionists and more moderate voters. But if he wanted to appeal to both groups, Lincoln would not be able to make any promises about bringing slavery to an end. Garrison faced a dilemma. Should he support Lincoln and hope that Herndon was being honest when he said that Lincoln opposed slavery?

Abraham Lincoln
(Courtesy of the Library of Congress)

Or should he continue to condemn all politicians as hopelessly corrupt?

While Garrison worried that Lincoln might not oppose slavery strongly enough, whites in the South feared that Lincoln was an outright abolitionist. Some southern politicians even vowed that the South would secede if Lincoln won the election. Democrats in the South nominated John C. Breckinridge, who wanted to extend slavery and make Cuba part of the United States. Democrats in the North nominated Stephen Douglas.

Only about 40 percent of American voters chose Lincoln on their ballots in the fall of 1860, and in the South he received virtually no support. Still, Lincoln won enough votes in the North to gain a majority in the Electoral College and with it the presidency. After the election returns came in, the country waited to see if southern states would follow through on their threat to secede.

Not surprisingly, South Carolina acted first. The state had always been outspoken when it came to the rights of slaveholders. In December 1860, South Carolina declared that it was seceding from the Union. By the time Lincoln took office in March 1861, six other states had followed South Carolina's lead. Together, the seven states formed a new government, the Confederate States of America, and named a wealthy plantation owner from Mississippi, Jefferson Davis, their president.

The first military confrontation between the Union and the newly formed Confederacy took place only about a month after Lincoln's inauguration. In April, Lincoln sent supplies to Fort Sumter, off the coast of South Carolina. The Confederacy took this as an act of war and fired upon the fort. The Union troops at the fort quickly surrendered, but just three days later Lincoln requested 75,000 volunteers to form an army to put down the rebellion. Angered by Lincoln's response, four states in the Upper South—Arkansas, North Carolina, Tennessee, and Virginia—seceded from the Union and joined the Confederacy. The Civil War had begun.

As men across the North signed up to answer Lincoln's call for soldiers, Garrison wondered what the war would bring. Would Lincoln free the slaves, or would he merely try to preserve the Union? At first, it was hard for the abolitionists to be optimistic. Lincoln said repeatedly that the purpose of the war was to bring the southern states back into the Union, not to bring slavery to an end. The abolitionists made it their goal to convince Lincoln and the North that the two sides could never have true peace until all the slaves were freed.

The abolitionists argued that freeing the slaves would have military benefits. It could deprive the South of millions of laborers. Abolitionists believed that if Lincoln declared the slaves free, it might inspire them to run away and even to help the North. Lincoln hesitated because he did not want to push the border states of Maryland, Missouri, Kentucky, and Delaware into the arms of the Confederacy. These four important states all allowed slavery, and there was still a risk that any of them, except perhaps Delaware, would choose to secede.

Most Northerners expected the war to end quickly, but they were soon disappointed. The North's larger population and stronger manufacturing gave it an edge, but to succeed, the North would have to invade the South. The South, by contrast, just had to outlast the will of the North to fight. In the summer of 1861, the South proved that it would not be easily defeated. Soldiers from North and South met in battle at Manassas, Virginia. The Union troops seemed to have the battle in hand, but Confederate reinforcements arrived, turning the battle into a decisive victory for the South. The defeat made it clear that the war would not be over soon.

As the war dragged on, the call to free the slaves grew louder. Petitions filled with the signatures of antislavery Northerners poured into Congress, and radical Republicans in the House and Senate tried to pass bills to end slavery. But President Lincoln continued to insist that the purpose of the war was to preserve the Union, not to end slavery.

Lincoln's hesitance to try to free the slaves disgusted most abolitionists. If the war would not bring an end to slavery, why sacrifice so many lives? Garrison grew worried that he had placed too much faith in Lincoln. When Union generals freed slaves in territory they had conquered, Lincoln responded by overturning their orders. He also tried to convince some free black Americans to move to Africa. Garrison could not believe that the president would support a colonization scheme. Garrison had fought hard against the American Colonization Society back in the 1830s, and he felt just as strongly about the issue now.

By the summer of 1862, things were going better for the North. Lincoln gradually became more confident that the border states would not join the rebels, and he began to think more seriously about freeing the slaves. After Union soldiers won an important victory in Maryland, Lincoln announced on September 22 that any slaves held in the rebellious states would be freed on January 1, 1863, unless the states returned to the Union.

Garrison was excited, but he was also disappointed that Lincoln's announcement seemed to exclude slaves held in border states. And, if the Confederate states ended the war, would slaveholders really be allowed to keep their slaves? He wrote to his daughter Fanny that "what is still needed, is a proclamation, distinctly announcing the total abolition of slavery." Other abolitionists complained that Lincoln still viewed emancipation as part of the war effort, rather than as a moral obligation.

Still, this was the closest the abolitionists had come to seeing an end to slavery. They knew that even if Lincoln's order was not perfect, it was still a big step. "The President's Proclamation is certainly matter for great rejoicing," Garrison admitted. Abolitionists across the North waited anxiously for New Year's Day to see if Lincoln would make good on his promise. Garrison and his family attended a concert that afternoon. In the middle of the event, news came that Lincoln had officially signed the Emancipation Proclamation: the slaves would be freed. The audience cheered the announcement, and then cried "Three cheers for Lincoln!" and "Three cheers for Garrison!"

Of course, there was still a war to win. With emancipation now an official purpose of the war, Garrison began printing reports of

Top: The storming of Fort Wagner *(Courtesy of the Library of Congress)* Bottom: The Battle of Olustee

President Abraham Lincoln and his Cabinet at the reading of the Emancipation Proclamation *(Courtesy of the Library of Congress)*

battles in the *Liberator.* Each victory on the battlefields was another step toward winning the war Garrison had been fighting for more than thirty years.

Soon after Lincoln issued his Emancipation Proclamation, he authorized the creation of regiments of black soldiers. In the spring of 1863, the Fifty-fourth Massachusetts regiment, composed of black soldiers and white officers, marched through a cheering crowd in Boston on its way to battlefields in the South. The Fifty-fourth later took part in a difficult siege of a fort in South Carolina in which more than half of the regiment's men died.

The creation of black regiments inspired George Garrison to take a more active role in the war effort. He had tried his hand at several careers, including apprenticeships as a clerk, accountant, and printer, but none had gone very well. He had worked off and on at the *Liberator* after returning from Kansas, but he never felt comfortable following in his father's footsteps.

During the Civil War, he had also drifted away from the pacifism of his parents, and now he saw an opportunity to make his own contribution to the effort to free the slaves.

George enlisted as an officer in a second black regiment, the Fifty-fifth Massachusetts regiment. As with the Fifty-fourth Massachusetts regiment, all the officers were white. Garrison and Helen tried to discourage George from joining the regiment. They worried that they might never see their son again. Garrison wrote his son a letter asking him to reconsider his decision. He wrote that he wished George were a pacifist,

A parchment replica of page one of the Emancipation Proclamation issued by President Lincoln on January 1, 1863

and he reminded George that, as the son of a famous abolitionist, George might face extra danger at the hands of the
Confederates if he were taken as a prisoner of war. Garrison
also wrote, "Your chance of being broken down by sickness,
wounded, maimed, or killed, in the course of such a prolonged
campaign, is indeed very great." Still, Garrison conceded,
"this is not a consideration to weigh heavily against the love
of liberty and the promptings of duty."

Garrison's final argument was that, if George were killed,
the loss would devastate George's poor mother. But like his
father, George was willing to risk his life for his belief in
a greater cause. George could not be convinced to change
his mind, so at about the same time that the Fifty-fourth
Massachusetts regiment went to battle in South Carolina, the
Garrison family saw George off to war.

George's brothers, Wendell and Willie, soon had to think
about whether they would go to war. Lincoln instituted a
draft lottery to raise more soldiers, and in the summer of 1863
Wendell was drafted. Drafted men had the option of paying a
fee of three hundred dollars instead of going to war. Wendell
believed that the war was for a good cause, but, unlike George,
he was still a pacifist. So Wendell chose to pay the fee rather
than fight himself. Willie's name was not called in the draft,
so he avoided having to make the difficult choice of whether
to go to war.

Their father was too old to fight, but he seemed as busy as
ever. In December 1863, he attended the thirtieth anniversary
meeting of the American Anti-Slavery Society in Philadelphia.
Times certainly had changed since that first meeting in 1833.
In his opening remarks, Garrison commented that it was
unlikely that the AAS would need a fortieth celebration in

another ten years, as it seemed that slavery would soon be brought to an end. Unlike thirty years earlier, no angry mobs threatened the lives of the abolitionists, and in fact much of the North seemed to be on their side. Senator Charles Sumner sent a letter to be read aloud at the gathering in which he celebrated their accomplishments, and other eminent attendees also praised Garrison and the abolitionists.

Garrison recalled how naive he had been to expect that the antislavery cause would be supported by his fellow citizens. "Instead of meeting with sympathy and encouragement," he said, "we had to face the frowns even of those who had formerly been our near and dear acquaintances!" In another speech, Garrison honored the memory of Benjamin Lundy, remembering how he had been inspired by reading Lundy's paper and hearing Lundy speak in Boston. Garrison joked that after he joined Lundy in Baltimore, "I drove off subscribers four or five times as fast as he could get them!"

For the most part, the gathering was more lighthearted than many past meetings, but there was one point of contention that caused quite a stir. Garrison believed that once the slaves were freed, the work of the AAS would be complete and the society could be disbanded. They were not there yet, he said, but it did not seem to be too far in the future. The first note of dissension came when Stephen Foster, a radical abolitionist from Ohio, reminded the audience that "there are two or three million of our countrymen yet clanking their heavy chains. While we are happy, they are sad and sorrowful. . . . Their fate is yet all uncertain." Foster worried that his fellow abolitionists had become too optimistic. It was still possible, he thought, that slavery would continue.

Other speakers followed Foster and said that although they agreed that there was still work to be done, things had improved. Surely there was reason to be more hopeful now. Part of the disagreement centered on how much faith to have in Lincoln. Foster argued that Lincoln had only issued the Emancipation Proclamation out of military necessity, not because he actually opposed slavery. Other speakers countered that Lincoln seemed to have changed his mind about slavery while in office, and that he was now committed to ending slavery. The dispute was a reminder of the many disagreements that had disrupted the movement since Garrison had first proposed the formation of the AAS years earlier.

Later in December, an event closer to home made these squabbles over tactics seem less important. On New Year's Eve, Helen suffered a stroke. For months afterward she could not get out of bed, leaving Fanny to manage the household.

Garrison stayed by his wife's side as much as possible, but work continued to call him away. In January, disagreement about whether to support Lincoln for reelection caused trouble at the annual meeting of the Massachusetts Anti-Slavery Society. Lincoln would have to run for reelection in the fall, and some of his critics in the abolitionist movement wanted to pass a resolution criticizing the president. Garrison proposed an amendment to the resolution that would make the language less harsh—a change from his usual endorsement of the strongest language possible—but his opponents, led by his close friend Wendell Phillips, defeated Garrison's amendment. Garrison and Phillips found themselves on opposite sides, and it proved hard to maintain their friendship as a result of this bitter dispute.

That summer, Garrison attended the Republican convention in Baltimore. He was happy to hear a number of speeches critical of slavery and to hear the audience cheer those criticisms. After the convention, he stopped in Washington, D.C., and met privately with President Lincoln. The meeting convinced Garrison that Lincoln opposed slavery and would do what he could to bring it to an end. Garrison wrote to Helen, "There is no mistake about it in regard to Mr. Lincoln's desire to do all that he can see it right and possible for him to do to uproot slavery."

When the votes were counted that fall, Lincoln won reelection, carrying every state except Kentucky, Delaware, and New Jersey. (The Confederate states did not take part in the election.) Garrison's faith in Lincoln proved well founded. On January 31, 1865, the House of Representatives approved the Thirteenth Amendment to the Constitution by a vote of 119 to 65. The amendment made slavery unconstitutional.

In April, the South surrendered, ending the Civil War. Garrison traveled to South Carolina, where he spoke to a large gathering at a black church. He also met with his son, who was stationed with his regiment nearby. But amid the celebration came devastating news: an assassin had shot and killed President Lincoln. Garrison rushed back to New York on April 21, where he grieved along with the rest of the North.

Thirty-Eighth **Congress of the United States of America;**

At the *Second* Session,

Begun and held at the City of Washington, on Monday, the *fifth* day of December, one thousand eight hundred and sixty-*four*

A RESOLUTION

Submitting to the legislatures of the several States a proposition to amend the Constitution of the United States.

Resolved by the Senate and House of Representatives of the United States of America in Congress assembled, (two-thirds of both houses concurring), That the following article be proposed to the legislatures of the several States as an amendment to the Constitution of the United States, which, when ratified by three-fourths of said Legislatures, shall be valid, to all intents and purposes, as a part of the said Constitution, namely: Article XIII. Section 1. Neither slavery nor involuntary servitude, except as a punishment for crime whereof the party shall have been duly convicted, shall exist within the United States, or any place subject to their jurisdiction. Section 2. Congress shall have power to enforce this article by appropriate legislation.

Schuyler Colfax
Speaker of the House of Representatives.

H. Hamlin
Vice President of the United States
and President of the Senate

Abraham Lincoln

Approved, February 1, 1865.

The Thirteenth Amendment to the U.S. Constitution

William Lloyd Garrison, publisher of the *Liberator*
(Courtesy of the Library of Congress)

Chapter
10

Grandfather Garrison

The war and slavery were now ended, but there were still questions about what freedom would mean. Blacks in both the North and South faced overwhelming racism from their fellow Americans. Across the South, states began passing laws restricting the rights of newly freed black men and women. Abolitionists now turned from the fight against slavery to the struggle for equality.

Garrison had been publishing his paper every week for more than thirty years, and he felt that it was time for him to move on. He decided to stop publishing the *Liberator* at the end of 1865. Other abolitionists wanted him to continue it or to let someone else take over the paper, but Garrison refused. He had started it, he said, and he had the right to stop publishing it. As the end of the year drew near, Garrison hoped that the Thirteenth Amendment would be officially ratified before the last issue of the *Liberator* was published. Finally, on December

18, 1865, the amendment became part of the Constitution—at last the Constitution no longer condoned slavery. Just over a week later, on December 29, Garrison published the final issue of his long-running paper.

As for the AAS, Garrison believed that it had served its purpose and should now be disbanded. Many members disagreed, and a majority voted to continue the organization. The official mission of the society became helping the freed slaves. Garrison resigned as president, and Wendell Phillips took his place.

Finally Garrison had more time to spend with his family. His children were grown, and Helen was not in the best of health. She never fully recovered from her stroke. Still, she continued to welcome guests into the house. She also wrote letters to her children and looked forward to their replies.

Two months after Helen's stroke, in February 1864, Willie became engaged to Ellen Wright, the daughter of abolitionists in New York. The two married that September, although Helen had not recovered enough to attend the ceremony. It was not long before Wendell married, too. Even Fanny was soon engaged, to a German journalist named Henry Villard. Villard liked to drink and smoke, which Fanny and her family did not like, but he agreed to give up these habits for his fiancée. They married early in 1866 and moved to Washington, D.C., and then New York City.

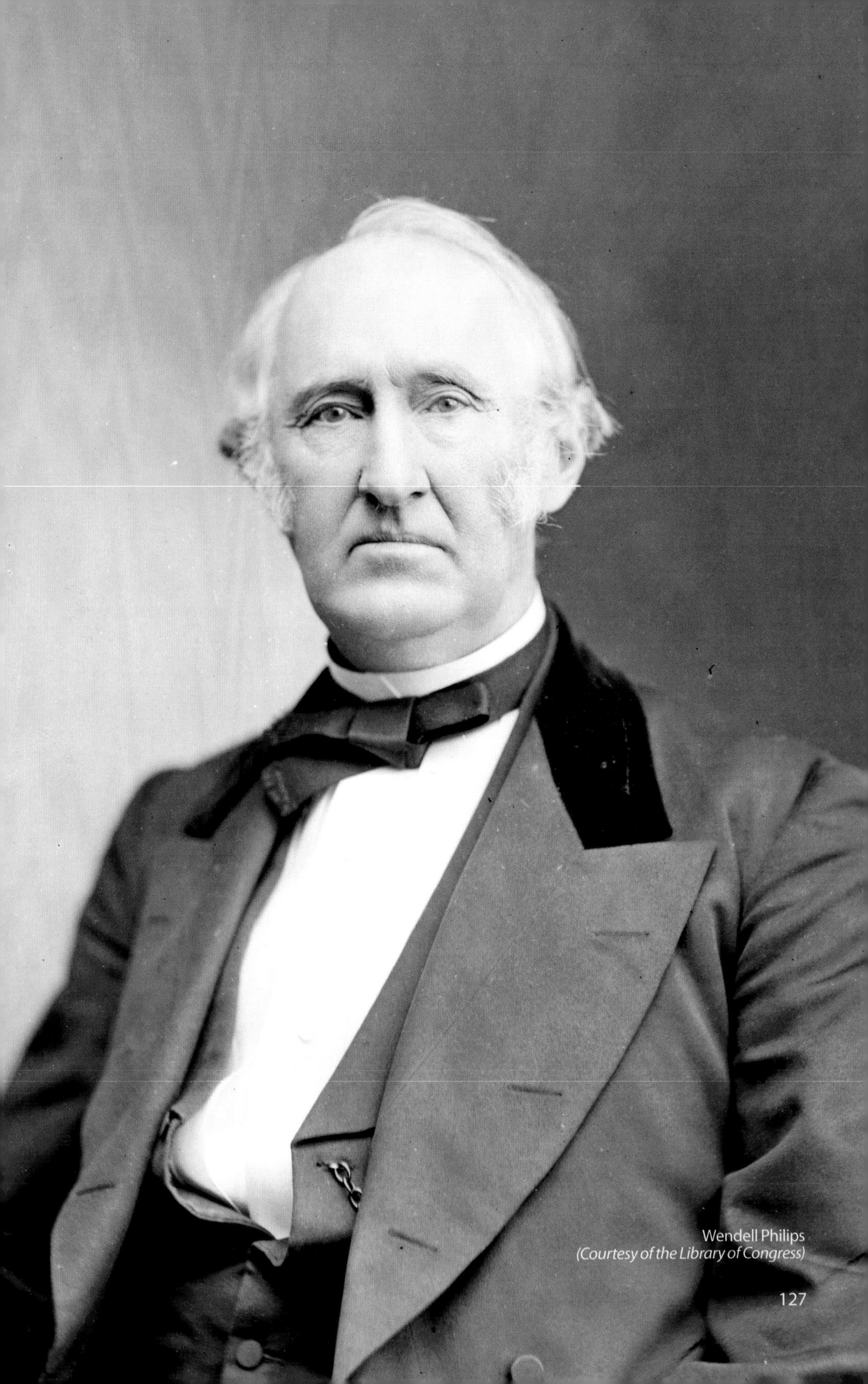

Wendell Philips
(Courtesy of the Library of Congress)

Garrison found ways to fill his time. He returned to England in 1867 to visit his friends from the abolitionist movement. He still did not handle ocean voyages well—as always, he got seasick—but he enjoyed the trip. After starting in England, Garrison continued on to France and Switzerland. Helen was not well enough to join him on the journey, but Garrison wrote her often, describing the crowded cities and the beauty of the Alps. After several months abroad, Garrison returned home.

Garrison also agreed to write a two-volume history of the abolitionist movement, but he soon found that he was not well suited to writing such long works. He had to return the advance he had been given, but fortunately friends had quietly managed to raise almost $30,000 dollars to support the Garrisons during their retirement. The gift recognized the enormous sacrifices Helen and Garrison had made in order to continue the battle against slavery. Garrison wrote to those who had donated money to thank them. "I shall try in vain to find words adequately to express my feelings," he wrote. Garrison also received a number of honors, including election to Phi Beta Kappa by Harvard. He was no longer a social outcast.

By 1868, Garrison was the proud grandfather of four young children. He wrote them letters and played with them when they

William Lloyd Garrison
(Courtesy of New York Public Library)

visited. They made him feel as if he were growing younger rather than older, he said.

Helen's health problems grew worse in the early 1870s. She had another stroke in 1871 and never fully regained her strength. Early in 1876, she caught a cold and became gravely ill. On January 25 of that year, Helen Garrison died. After her death, Garrison relied heavily on his children, particularly Frank. He had trouble knowing quite what to do with himself without his wife there at his side. "I wander from room to room in a state of bewilderment," he wrote to his son Wendell. "Outwardly and inwardly she was loveliness itself. She captivated me as soon as I became acquainted with her." Garrison told Wendell that Fanny had recently discovered a pile of letters written by Helen during their courtship. Garrison read them over and over again. They still excited him as much now as they had in 1834.

Throughout the 1870s, Garrison wrote to old friends, often discussing other members of the abolitionist movement who had recently died. He congratulated John Greenleaf Whittier on his seventieth birthday. "Less than a score of years ago, neither of us expected to live to see the abolition of chattel slavery in our land," Garrison wrote.

Of course, Garrison did not entirely abandon his public life. He did not attend as many meetings and conventions as he once had, but he played an active role in the women's movement. He also wrote fiery letters about politics to the editors of newspapers. When Congress debated a bill that would limit immigration from China, Garrison furiously condemned the bill in the *New York Tribune*. He then wrote to Fanny to say that he expected he would get quite a bit of criticism for his letter, but he did not mind. After all, he said, his years of anti-slavery work had taught him not to worry about criticism.

Oswald Villard, 1930
(Courtesy of German Federal Archive)

On March 12, 1879, Garrison wrote a letter to his grandson Oswald Garrison Villard, one of Fanny's children. Oswald, who grew up admiring his grandfather, would later become one of the founders of the National Association for the Advancement of Colored People (NAACP), an organization dedicated to ensuring the civil rights of black Americans. Garrison wished Oswald a happy seventh birthday and apologized for not being able to make it to his party. As always, Garrison had advice to offer:

You are now able to go to school, but there are many lessons to learn besides those which are taught in the school-books. The most important relate to our conduct through life. The act which is wrong in itself we must never do, but always stand up for the right. Never do to another, not even in play, what you would not have him do to you. Avoid all quarrelling, be kind and obliging to others, love and honor your parents, pity the poor and suffering, and in all things try to do the very best in your power.

In April, Garrison became involved in an effort to raise money to help resettle black Americans who had been forced to leave the South because of violence by whites.

Vigilante groups such as the Ku Klux Klan had formed across the South in the years after the Civil War. These groups claimed to protect white Southerners from black criminals, but in reality the blacks they caught and murdered rarely had committed any crime. Instead, whites used violence to maintain political and economic control of the South.

Garrison had become ill suddenly, so he could not attend a meeting held by the fundraising committee, but he wrote a letter to be read at the meeting. Violence against blacks in the South was making a mockery of the American government, he wrote. "It is clear, therefore, that the battle of liberty and equal rights is to be fought over again."

By May, Garrison's illness grew more serious. It soon appeared that he would not recover. Fanny convinced him to stay with her so that she could care for him, and his sons also gathered in New York City later that month to be with their father during his final days. The house was full when, late at night on May 24, 1879, William Lloyd Garrison died.

The large crowd that gathered to honor Garrison after his death reflected the changes that he had helped bring about through his years of relentless agitation. A public memorial was held at a church in Roxbury, Massachusetts, and flags across the state flew at half-mast on May 28, the day of his funeral.

Just after two that afternoon, pallbearers carried his casket into the church. Before his death, Garrison had made it clear that he did not want his funeral to be a mournful occasion, so the church blinds remained open to let in the spring sunshine as the mourners sang some of Garrison's favorite hymns. The minister began the service by remarking how wonderful it was that Garrison, who not many years before had been "regarded as all that was dangerous and destructive" was now "well-nigh universally regarded with enthusiastic admiration." A number of speakers mentioned how warm and welcoming Garrison had always been in person, despite his fearsome reputation.

Garrison's old friend Wendell Phillips also spoke. The two had reconciled their differences as they grew older, and Phillips now recalled the enormous changes that had taken place over the past fifty years. He pointed out that, at the time

Aerial view of New York City
(Courtesy of Photo Art Collection (PAC)/Alamy)

Garrison started his crusade, the idea of immediate emancipation seemed both impossible and utterly insane to almost every other white American. But that had never stopped him, Phillips said. Garrison had been the conscience of the nation. Decades of indifference and condemnation had only made Garrison more determined to make himself heard. And in the end, he had been right.

133

Timeline

1805 | Born in Newburyport, Massachusetts, on December 12.

1815 | Moves to Baltimore with mother and brother; returns to Massachusetts and begins an apprenticeship to a cabinetmaker.

1818 | Begins his apprenticeship at the *Newburyport Herald.*

1822 | Begins to submit newspaper essays under the pseudonym "An Old Bachelor."

1825 | Apprenticeship at *Newburyport Herald* ends in December.

1829 | Gives his first address against slavery; becomes co-editor of the *Genius of Universal Emancipation* and publishes first issue on September 2.

1830 | Serves seven weeks in jail after a slave trader successfully sued him for libel.

1831 | Publishes the first issue of the *Liberator* on January 1.

1832 | Founds the New England Anti-Slavery Society

1833 | Co-founds the American Anti-Slavery Society; visits England.

1834 | Marries Helen Benson in Brooklyn, Connecticut, on September 4.

1835 | Dragged through the streets of Boston to City Hall by an angry mob.

1836 | Son George Thompson born, first of seven children.

1838 | Son William "Willie" Lloyd Jr. born.

1840 Son Wendell "Wendy" Phillips born.

1841 Meets escaped slave Frederick Douglass.

1842 Son Charles Follen born.

1844 First daughter, Helen "Fanny" Frances, born.

1846 Second daughter Elizabeth "Lizzy" Pease born; dies two years later.

1848 Son Francis Jackson born.

1849 Son Charles Follen dies.

1850 Denounces the Compromise of 1850, which includes a stronger fugitive slave law.

1854 Burns a copy of the Constitution while giving a speech at an antislavery rally in Framingham, Massachusetts; denounces the Kansas-Nebraska Act.

1859 Hails John Brown's raid on Harper's Ferry.

1865 Publishes the final issue of the *Liberator* on December 29, after passage of the Thirteenth Amendment and two years after Abraham Lincoln issues the Emancipation Proclamation.

1879 Dies on May 24 in New York City.

Sources

Chapter One: Growing Up Fast

p. 16,   "and not trouble myself . . ." William Lloyd Garrison, *The Letters of William Lloyd Garrison,* vol. I: *I Will Be Heard*, ed. Walter M. Merrill (Cambridge: The Belknap Press of Harvard University Press, 1971), 6.

p. 17,   "instead of the tall . . ." Ibid., 14.

Chapter Two: From Journalist to Abolitionist

p. 25,   "My very knees . . ." Garrison, *Letters,* vol. I, 83.

p. 25,   "Our politics are rotten . . ." George Frederickson, ed., *William Lloyd Garrison* (Englewood Cliffs, NJ: Prentice Hall, 1968), 13-19.

p. 26,   "The nation will . . ." Frederickson, William Lloyd Garrison, 19.

p. 26,   "It was plain truth . . ." Garrison, *Letters,* vol. I, 84.

p.. 27-28, "Any man can gather . . ." William Lloyd Garrison, in *Against Wind and Tide: A Biography of Wm. Lloyd Garrison* (Cambridge: Harvard University Press, 1963), 33.

p. 29,   "I hold no fellowship . . ." Garrison, *Letters,* vol. I, 113.

Chapter Three: The Liberator

p. 34,   "lift up the standard . . ." Frances Jackson Garrison and Wendell Phillips Garrison, *William Lloyd Garrison 1805-1879: The Story of His Life Told by His Children*, vols. 1-4 (New York: The Century Company, 1885-1889), 224.

p. 34-35, "I am in earnest . . ." Frederickson, *William Lloyd Garrison*, 22-23.

p. 36,   "the public imagine[s] . . ." Garrison, *Letters,* vol. I, 114.

Chapter Four: Courtship and Courting Danger

p. 47,   "Have you any thing . . ." Garrison, Garrison, *Letters,* vol. I, 289.

p. 47-48, "Yes, my fears . . ." Ibid., 303.

p. 48,   "Do I think of you . . ." Ibid., 336.

p. 48,   "I did not marry her . . ." Ibid., 493.

p. 50,   "My mind is . . ." Ibid., 530.

p. 52,   "the most disgraceful event . . ." William Lloyd Garrison, *Selections from the Writings and Speeches of William Lloyd Garrison* (Boston: R. F. Wallcut, 1852), 391.

p. 52, "A mob in Boston . . ." George Thompson, *Letters and Addresses by George Thompson, During His Mission in the United States* (Boston: Isaac Knapp, 1837), 100.

p. 52, "New subscribers . . ." Garrison, *Letters,* vol. I, 552.

Chapter Five: Dissension in the Ranks

p. 61, "I read *The Philanthropist* . . ." William Lloyd Garrison, *The Letters of William Lloyd Garrison,* vol. II: *A House Dividing Against Itself, 1836-1840,* ed. Louis Ruchames (Cambridge: The Belknap Press of Harvard University Press, 1971), 67.

p. 62, "It cannot be disguised . . ." Francis Jackson, *Letters,* vol. II, 577.

p. 63, "a glorious triumph . . ." Garrison, *Letters,* vol. II, 611.

p. 65, "So! I am now . . ." Ibid., 660.

Chapter Six: A Call for Disunion

p. 68, "I shall never forget . . ." Garrison, preface to Frederick Douglass, *Narrative of the Life of Frederick Douglass, an American Slave, Written by Himself* (New York: Signet, 1997), 4.

p. 74, "Three millions of the . . ." Garrison in Frederickson, ed., *William Lloyd Garrison,* 53.

p. 76, "greatest crime of his age . . ." William Lloyd Garrison, *The Letters of William Lloyd Garrison,* vol. III, *No Union with Slaveholders, 1841-1849,* ed. Walter M. Merrill (Cambridge: The Belknap Press of Harvard University Press, 1973, 300.

p. 77, "In hottest . . ." Frederick Douglass, *Narrative of the Life of Frederick Douglass, an American Slave. Written by Himself.* (General Books LLC, 2009), 30.

Chapter Seven: The Consequences of Compromise

p. 85, "For a month past . . ." Garrison, *Letters,* vol. III, 550.

p. 85, "He became perfectly . . ." Ibid., 620.

p. 85, "a staggering blow . . ." Ibid., 619.

Chapter Eight: Lighting the Match

p. 98, "My language was strong . . ." William Lloyd Garrison, *The Letters of William Lloyd Garrison,* vol. IV: *From Disunionism to the Brink of War, 1850-1860,* ed. Louis Ruchames (Cambridge: The Belknap Press of Harvard University Press, 1975), 292.

p. 99, "was formed at the expense . . ." Garrison, *Selections*, 308.

p. 99, "It is absurd . . ." Ibid., 311.

p. 101, "Is it not plain . . ." Garrison, the *Liberator*, March 14. 1856.

p. 106, "For all our efforts . . ." Garrison, *Letters,* vol. IV, 454.

Chapter Nine: War!

p. 110, "Upon the face of it . . ." Garrison, *Letters,* vol. IV, 664.

p. 110, "Now, if it is deemed . . ." John Brown, *The Life and Letters of John Brown: Liberator of Kansas and Martyr of Virginia* (Boston: Roberts Brothers, 1891), 585.

p. 116, "what is still needed . . ." William Lloyd Garrison, *The Letters of William Lloyd Garrison,* vol. V: *Let the Oppressed Go Free, 1861-1867,* ed. Walter M. Merrill (Cambridge: The Belknap Press of Harvard University Press, 1979), 114.

p. 116, "The President's Proclamation . . ." Ibid., 114.

p. 119, "Your chance of being . . ." Ibid., 160.

p. 120, "Instead of meeting with . . ." William Lloyd Garrison, *The Anti-Slavery Crusade in America: Proceedings of the American Anti-Slavery Society at Its Third Decade* (New York: Arno Press, 1969), 25.

p. 120, "I drove off . . ." Ibid., 121.

p. 120, "there are two or three . . ." Ibid., 57.

p. 122, "There is no mistake . . ." Garrison, *Letters,* vol. V, 212.

Chapter Ten: Grandfather Garrison

p. 128, "I shall try in vain . . ." William Lloyd Garrison, *The Letters of William Lloyd Garrison,* vol. VI: *To Rouse the Slumbering Land, 1868-1879,* eds. Walter M. Merrill and Louis Ruchames (Cambridge: The Belknap Press of Harvard University Press, 1981), 41.

p. 129, "I wander from . . ." Ibid., 400-401.

p. 129, "Less than a score . . ." Ibid., 491.

p. 130, "You are now able . . ." Ibid., 568.

p. 131, "It is clear . . ." Ibid., 580.

p. 131, "regarded as all . . ." *Tributes to William Lloyd Garrison at the Funeral Services, May 28, 1879* (Boston: Houghton, Osgood and Company, 1879), 21.

Bibliography

Alonso, Harriet Hyman. *Growing Up Abolitionist: The Story of the Garrison Children*. Amherst, Mass.: University of Massachusetts Press, 2002.

Frederickson, George M., ed. *William Lloyd Garrison*. Englewood Cliffs, NJ: Prentice Hall, 1968.

Garrison, Francis Jackson, and Wendell Phillips Garrison. *William Lloyd Garrison, 1805-1879: The Story of His Life Told by His Children*, vols. 1-4. New York: The Century Company, 1885-1889.

Mayer, Henry. *All on Fire: William Lloyd Garrison and the Abolition of Slavery*. New York: St. Martin's Press, 1998.

McPherson, James M. *Battle Cry of Freedom: The Civil War Era*. New York: Ballantine Books, 1988.

Merrill, Walter M. *Against Wind and Tide: A Biography of William Lloyd Garrison*. Cambridge: Harvard University Press, 1963.

Nelson, Truman, ed. *Documents of Upheaval: Selections from William Lloyd Garrison's The Liberator, 1831-1865*. New York: Hill and Wang, 1966.

Stewart, James B. *Holy Warriors: The Abolitionists and American Slavery*. New York: Hill and Wang, 1996.

Web sites

http://www.pbs.org/wgbh/aia/part4/4p1561.html
A biography of Garrison is featured on this PBS (Public Broadcasting Service) site, as well as links to a letter to Garrison from Harriet Beecher Stowe and an editorial entitled "To the Public," which appeared in the first issue of the *Liberator*.

http://www.theliberatorfiles.com
On this Web site, developed by National Park ranger Horace Sheldon, visitors will find a collection of articles that appeared in the *Liberator* from 1831 to 1879. There are also links to images relevant to the life of Garrison.

Book cover and interior design by Derrick Carroll

Index